The Kentucky Bicentennial Bookshelf
Sponsored by

KENTUCKY HISTORICAL EVENTS CELEBRATION COMMISSION
KENTUCKY FEDERATION OF WOMEN'S CLUBS

and Contributing Sponsors

AMERICAN FEDERAL SAVINGS & LOAN ASSOCIATION
ARMCO STEEL CORPORATION, ASHLAND WORKS
A. ARNOLD & SON TRANSFER & STORAGE CO., INC. / ASHLAND OIL, INC.
BAILEY MINING COMPANY, BYPRO, KENTUCKY / BEGLEY DRUG COMPANY
J. WINSTON COLEMAN, JR. / CONVENIENT INDUSTRIES OF AMERICA, INC.
IN MEMORY OF MR. AND MRS. J. SHERMAN COOPER BY THEIR CHILDREN
CORNING GLASS WORKS FOUNDATION / MRS. CLORA CORRELL
THE COURIER-JOURNAL AND THE LOUISVILLE TIMES
COVINGTON TRUST & BANKING COMPANY
MR. AND MRS. GEORGE P. CROUNSE / GEORGE E. EVANS, JR.
FARMERS BANK & CAPITAL TRUST COMPANY / FISHER-PRICE TOYS, MURRAY
MARY PAULINE FOX, M.D., IN HONOR OF CHLOE GIFFORD
MARY A. HALL, M.D., IN HONOR OF PAT LEE,
JANICE HALL & MARY ANN FAULKNER
OSCAR HORNSBY INC. / OFFICE PRODUCTS DIVISION IBM CORPORATION
JERRY'S RESTAURANTS / ROBERT B. JEWELL
LEE S. JONES / KENTUCKIANA GIRL SCOUT COUNCIL
KENTUCKY BANKERS ASSOCIATION / KENTUCKY COAL ASSOCIATION, INC.
THE KENTUCKY JOCKEY CLUB, INC. / THE LEXINGTON WOMAN'S CLUB
LINCOLN INCOME LIFE INSURANCE COMPANY
LORILLARD A DIVISION OF LOEW'S THEATRES, INC.
METROPOLITAN WOMAN'S CLUB OF LEXINGTON / BETTY HAGGIN MOLLOY
MUTUAL FEDERAL SAVINGS & LOAN ASSOCIATION
NATIONAL INDUSTRIES, INC. / RAND MCNALLY & COMPANY
PHILIP MORRIS, INCORPORATED / MRS. VICTOR SAMS
SHELL OIL COMPANY, LOUISVILLE
SOUTH CENTRAL BELL TELEPHONE COMPANY
SOUTHERN BELLE DAIRY CO. INC.
STANDARD OIL COMPANY (KENTUCKY)
STANDARD PRINTING CO., H. M. KESSLER, PRESIDENT
STATE BANK & TRUST COMPANY, RICHMOND
THOMAS INDUSTRIES INC. / TIP TOP COAL CO., INC.
MARY L. WISS, M.D. / YOUNGER WOMAN'S CLUB OF ST. MATTHEWS

Proud Kentuckian

John C. Breckinridge

1821-1875

FRANK H. HECK

THE UNIVERSITY PRESS OF KENTUCKY

Research for The Kentucky Bicentennial Bookshelf
is assisted by a grant from the
National Endowment for the Humanities.
Views expressed in the Bookshelf do not
necessarily represent those of the Endowment.

ISBN: 0-8131-0217-0

Library of Congress Catalog Card Number: 76-9502

Editorial and Sales Offices: Lexington, Kentucky 40506

Contents

Acknowledgments

IT IS IMPOSSIBLE to express adequately my gratitude to all who helped in some way with the writing of this book. A grant-in-aid allocated by the Carnegie Research Committee from funds made available jointly by the Carnegie Foundation and Centre College of Kentucky partly financed my first plunge, more than twenty years ago, into the sources for the life of John C. Breckinridge. That adventure resulted in an article published in the *Journal of Southern History,* which, considerably modified, serves as the foundation for this book's chapter on "The Crisis of Disunion." Portions of the article are used here by permission of the *Journal of Southern History.* In more recent years my Breckinridge studies have been encouraged by several grants-in-aid for summer research made by Centre College on the recommendation of the Council on Faculty Development.

I am grateful for the helpful cooperation of staff members of the Manuscript Division of the Library of Congress, the National Archives, the Lexington (Kentucky) Public Library, the Free Public Library of Burlington, Iowa, the Kornhauser Health Services Library of the University of Louisville, and the libraries of the University of Kentucky, Transylvania University, Centre College, the University of Chicago, Princeton University, the Filson Club, Louisville, the Kentucky Historical Society, Frankfort, the Iowa State Department of History and Archives, Des Moines, the Chicago Historical Society, the Cincinnati Historical Society, the Western Reserve Historical Society, Cleveland, and the Historical Society of Pennsylvania, Philadelphia. I am particularly indebted in this regard to my former student, James R. Bentley, curator of manuscripts and secretary of the Filson Club, and to Dr. Jacqueline Bull, head of Special Collections in the library of the University of Kentucky.

Helpful also were personnel of the offices of the Recorder of Deeds, Washington, D.C., and the county clerks of Boyle, Fayette, and Scott counties, Kentucky, and Des Moines County, Iowa. My colleague, Professor E. W. Cook, Jr., longtime clerk of the Session of the Second Presbyterian Church, Danville, Kentucky, gave me access to the antebellum records of the Presbyterian Churches of Danville. Mrs. James Carson Breckinridge of Summit Point, West Virginia, graciously provided a photograph of a portrait of Mary Cyrene Breckinridge which she owns. As I was finishing my work, Dr. James C. Klotter kindly lent me a personal copy of his unpublished dissertation, "The Breckinridges of Kentucky: Two Centuries of Leadership" (University of Kentucky, 1975), a study which provided some useful insights.

In a class by themselves are Mr. and Mrs. John Marshall Prewitt and Mrs. Clifton R. Breckinridge of Mt. Sterling, Kentucky. They not only made available the treasures in their personal collection and shared their knowledge of family traditions, but also gave marked encouragement as the study progressed. Also helpful was Mrs. Evan McCord of Versailles, Kentucky.

For their critical reading of a draft of the manuscript, I record my hearty thanks to my colleague, Professor Charles R. Lee, Jr., and my son, Edward V. Heck. Professor Holman Hamilton of the University of Kentucky kindly gave his opinion on a controversial passage. The criticism of my colleague, Professor Charles T. Hazelrigg, improved the style of the chapter which he was good enough to read.

An excellent case could be made for naming my wife, Edna Drill Heck, as coauthor. In any event I acknowledge with deep appreciation her service as a research associate, particularly as we worked together at the Library of Congress and the library of the University of Chicago. She has read so many nineteenth-century Breckinridge letters that she has developed a first-name involvement with Breckinridges long gone. Throughout the years of my interest in John C. Breckinridge she has been my soundest and altogether best critic. Readers will understand, however, that neither she nor the friends whom I have named should be charged with any flaws they may find in the volume now before them.

Introduction

THIS LITTLE VOLUME is devoted to the short life of one of the most eminent Kentuckians of his generation, a man whom friends and acquaintances found singularly fascinating. Now, a hundred years after his death, the secret of John Cabell Breckinridge's charm is hard to recover. No doubt it was compounded of many things: an erect, manly, athletic figure, tall by the standards of his day, impressive on foot and doubly so when mounted; a genuine and considerate interest in all sorts and conditions of people, evidenced by word and deed from childhood until the last week of his life and enhanced by the successful politician's gift for linking names and faces; unusual tact; piercing blue eyes; a quick mind and a rich, resonant speaking voice. Few photographs of Breckinridge reveal the handsome man described by virtually everyone whose comments on his appearance survive. But antebellum photography was at best something of an ordeal, and the conventions of the time required a public man to appear grave if not stern. Thus photographic portraits do not reflect Breckinridge's warm smile, hearty laugh, firm handclasp, or gifts as a raconteur, for all of which there is abundant written evidence. Nor can they show his sense of humor, reported in the youthful letters of his sister Laetitia and certain of his college mates, and revealed in the letters which he himself wrote a favorite son in later years.

Breckinridge's life spanned almost exactly the second of the four half-centuries which have passed since the permanent settlement of Kentucky by white men and women and their black slaves. It was a half-century of tremendous growth and far-reaching change. When Breckinridge was born in 1821, the population of the United States totaled less than ten million people. Kentucky, sixth in order of population among the twenty-three states of the Union, had nearly 575,000. At his death in 1875, his native state boasted some 1,450,000 inhabitants, while the whole country could claim approximately 43,000,000. When he was born, primitive river steamboats and fleet horses were the fastest means of travel known; not a mile of steam railroad was in service anywhere in the United States. When he died, some 73,000 miles of railroad were in operation within the bounds of the republic, and no thinking person could deny that railroads were the key to the nation's economy and to much else in the life of her people.

Breckinridge's fifty-four years fell into four obvious divisions. The first embraced his childhood and young manhood, until his first election to public office in August, 1849, at the age of twenty-eight. It included his preparation for a career in law, his early progress in that career, and his few months as a volunteer officer during the latter stages of the War with Mexico. The second period of a dozen years included a short and meteoric career in politics, extending from his election to the Kentucky House of Representatives through his two terms as a member of the federal House of Representatives, his four years as vice president of the United States, his election as a United States senator, his candidacy for the presidency, and his resignation from the Senate in October, 1861. The third division, much the most dramatic, was also the most brief—3½ years as a general officer in the army of the Confederate States of America, concluding with a few short weeks as secretary of war when the cause was already lost. The final and anticlimactic period lasted almost exactly a decade. Opened by an exciting and exhausting escape from the victorious forces of the United States, it included nearly four years of exile in Canada and Europe and a quiet return to Kentucky in 1869, followed by six years devoted to the practice of law and an effort to promote railroad building in central Kentucky.

Breckinridge in many ways was conventional, not to say conservative, in his thinking. But the career of a man who was elected vice president of the United States during the first year in which he was eligible to hold that office, evidencing a precocity that has not yet been equaled, calls for attention. His wartime role was more than exciting. As a former vice president he was the highest ranking officer of the United States to play an active part as a combat commander in the army of the Confederate States. He was the most eminent Kentuckian to cast his lot with the Confederacy, while his respected uncle, Robert Breckinridge, was one of the most influential Kentuckians who struggled to keep Kentucky loyal to the Union. What better illustration can be found of the trauma of the Brothers' War in a border state?

1

YEARS OF PREPARATION

JOHN CABELL BRECKINRIDGE was born on January 16, 1821, into a family which had a sound basis for the keen sense of family pride which was one of its distinctive marks. His paternal grandfather, John Breckinridge, had moved from Albemarle County, Virginia, to Kentucky in 1793 at the age of thirty-three. During his remaining thirteen years he amassed a large landed estate, developed a rich Bluegrass farm devoted to diversified agriculture and stock raising, and attained a position as a recognized leader of the Kentucky bar. He served from 1793 until 1797 as attorney general of Kentucky. In 1798 he introduced into the Kentucky House of Representatives the famed Kentucky Resolutions, which denounced the Alien and Sedition Acts as an unconstitutional usurpation of power by Congress and invited the other states to join Kentucky in declaring the offending measures "void and of no force." Thus he took his stand as a high priest of states rights dogma and of strict construction of the Constitution. In 1799 he played a leading part in the convention which wrote Kentucky's second constitution. Twice Speaker of the Kentucky House of Representatives, he was elected in November 1800 to represent his adopted state in the United States Senate. After four years, 1801–05, as a vigorous and effective leader of President Jefferson's supporters in that body, he accepted the president's proffer of appointment as attorney general of the United States. He still held this position when he died in December, 1806.[1]

The eldest son of Attorney General Breckinridge and his wife, Mary Hopkins Cabell (Polly to her contemporaries), was Joseph Cabell, whom the family called by his middle name. After graduation in 1810 from the College of New Jersey at Princeton, he studied law and in 1814 was admitted to the bar. Settling in Lexington, he quickly built up an extensive practice in both state and federal courts. An unusually handsome young man, he was already thirty-two years old when his only son, John Cabell, was born. By that time he had served three terms in the Kentucky House of Representatives, the last two as its Speaker. In 1820 Gov. John Adair appointed him secretary of state.

Cabell Breckinridge's wife, Mary Clay Smith, had an equally proud lineage. She was a daughter of Samuel Stanhope Smith, professor at the College of New Jersey after 1779 and president of that institution from 1795 until 1812. Smith was a tall, handsome man with a sonorous voice and a high reputation as a pulpit orator. In early manhood he had married Ann Witherspoon, daughter of John Witherspoon, his immediate predecessor as president. Witherspoon, brought from Scotland in 1768 to be president of the college and pastor of the First Presbyterian Church of Princeton, represented New Jersey intermittently from 1776 until 1782 in the Continental Congress. A signer of the Declaration of Independence, he was famed for his advocacy of complete religious liberty. He played an important role in the series of meetings which led in 1789 to the establishment of the General Assembly of the Presbyterian Church in the United States of America. Appropriately, he was chosen its first moderator.

John Cabell's parents fell in love during his father's student days at Princeton. In the spring of 1811, taking his sister Mary Ann with him to represent his family, Cabell returned to New Jersey to claim his bride. The wedding on May 11 was followed by a round of social engagements in Princeton, Philadelphia, and New York. In August, after a long, painful journey by carriage and horseback across the Pennsylvania mountains and southern Ohio, the couple reached Cabell's Dale, the home which the bridegroom's father had built in Fayette County six miles north of Lexington. There his strong-willed mother, wearing her black widow's cap in lieu of a crown, reigned supreme. And there the weary travelers experienced five days of the hilarious noise and mirth with which Kentucky weddings were celebrated in those days.

In little more than nine months after the wedding day, the young couple welcomed their first daughter, Frances. The second, born in October, 1813, was named Caroline; and a third, Mary, put in her appearance in January, 1815. Six years intervened between her birth and that of the son. Twenty months after John's birth his sister Laetitia was born.

The birth of a son to a mother who had been married nearly ten years and had not produced a living child for six was the occasion of much rejoicing. The boy was born at Thorn Hill, a handsome but heavily mortgaged home in Lexington which his father had purchased six years earlier from John W. Hunt. Less than four months after his birth the parents brought their son to be baptized at the Market Street (McChord's) Presbyterian Church, where Cabell Breckinridge was a ruling elder and both his wife and mother were members.

Shortly thereafter Cabell moved his family to Frankfort, where they made their home for a little more than two years. There in August, 1823, a visiting cousin from Virginia and other members of the household were taken ill with a serious malady described in contemporary newspapers and family correspondence only as "the prevailing fever." Cabell took his five young children for safety to his mother's home and then returned to help care for his guest, who presently recovered. But Cabell and his wife were soon stricken with the same ailment; after hardly a week's illness, he died early on September 1, 1823. That evening friends carried his body to Cabell's Dale for interment. It was some days before his distracted widow was well enough to join her children there and three weeks before she could think of anything but her bereavement.

The death of the handsome and eloquent young secretary of state was widely regretted as a loss to the commonwealth. For his family it could not have come at a more unfortunate time. His simple will, executed in 1816, made his wife his only heir and executrix. But as a brother-in-law, David Castleman, wrote Cabell's brother Robert, "It is scarcely necessary to say to you that his estate is very much embarrassed." Cabell's scale of living in Lexington and Frankfort had seemed unduly lavish to his thrifty, though devoted, mother. Debts amounting to not less than $25,000 were far from balanced by uncollected professional fees and salary, two unsalable houses and lots in Lexington, household furniture and personal effects, one male slave, and the personal and legal library of the deceased. Furthermore the estate of Attorney General John Breckinridge, who had died seventeen years earlier, was still unsettled and tied up in litigation. But Cabell's share, even after proper allowance was made for his legal services as trustee of the estate, had been largely dissipated by the advances he had received and the debts he had contracted.

Had Cabell died in a time of general prosperity, more could have been realized from his estate; but his death came at a moment when Kentucky and the country at large were suffering from the prolonged depression which followed the Panic of 1819. His brother Robert, who hastily completed his preparation for the bar, assumed the chief responsibility for meeting the late secretary of state's obligations and settling his estate. He carried that heavy burden until in 1832 he entered the

Presbyterian ministry as pastor of a church in Baltimore previously served by his brother John.

Not surprisingly, Cabell's high-strung and well-read widow found it hard to believe that her brother-in-law had done the best he could for her or to understand that it had not been possible from the ruins of her husband's estate to save enough to enable her to live independently, if not in the generous style to which she had become accustomed. For several years she was virtually dependent upon her mother-in-law for a residence, the food which she and her children ate, and the clothing which they wore. As time went on, bruised feelings resulted in an open clash between the two proud and durable widows.[2] The elder, "Grandma Black-Cap" to the younger generation, came to think the worst of her daughter-in-law. That lady in turn hated Robert with all her might and taught her children that he had wronged her and them.

Yet the most important influences in young John's first twelve years were without doubt his mother and his grandmother. Growing up in an atmosphere of suspicion and tension, he might have become bitter and sullen. Instead, responding to the necessities of the situation, he developed before manhood a degree of tact unusual in one of his years.

Meanwhile he learned his letters and enjoyed the amusements open to a lad who lived on a large, rural estate. Indian artifacts, found in abundance in a corner of the Cabell's Dale property, early fascinated him and aroused a lifelong interest in the American Indian. He experienced such common childhood diseases as mumps and measles. In November 1829, when he was nearly nine, he saw his eldest sister, Frances, married to the Reverend John Clarke Young, pastor of the Market Street Presbyterian Church. Less than a year later Young, a mere twenty-seven years of age, accepted the presidency of struggling Centre College at Danville, thirty-five miles from Lexington. When John was ten, his Uncle Robert's wife, Sophonisba Preston, writing a distant aunt, reported his recovery from an unidentified ailment and added that he "is a fine boy, smart and amiable." In January, 1832, barely eleven years old, he witnessed the marriage of his sister Mary, his senior by only six years, to Dr. Thomas P. Satterwhite, a prominent Lexington physician.

Later that year, the breach between John's mother and grandmother now complete, the former moved to Danville, where she made her home with the Youngs. In the nature of things, John and Laetitia moved with her. In 1835 she was called back to Lexington by the death of Mary Satterwhite, three weeks after she had given birth to her second child, a son named for his father. For nearly ten years thereafter she remained in the Satterwhite household, caring for her orphaned grandchildren. But from 1832 until his graduation as a bachelor of arts in September, 1838, John lived and studied, except during vacations, in the home of President Young on the campus of Centre College.

Young, with John's mother and grandmother, was to prove one of the principal influences on the developing lad. Though the three differed radically in personality and manner, they all taught him a strict morality, rooted in a Presbyterian reading of Holy Writ. All three prayed that he might be a worthy representative of his proud heritage. And all three exhorted him to make full use of his native talents.

The raw young institution over which Young presided and in which his youthful brother-in-law enrolled had been chartered less than two years before John's birth. When he entered, his fellow students numbered about 100; by his final term the enrollment had risen to 150. Of that total, half were members of one of the four regular classes and were candidates for the bachelor of arts degree. About a third were preparatory school students, and the rest were "irregulars" or special students. A large majority were Kentuckians, but 45 came from else-where—a half dozen from New York, but most of the others from Florida territory and the states south and southeast of Kentucky.

After two years in the grammar school or preparatory department of the college, John had learned enough Latin and Greek, English grammar, arithmetic, and geography to qualify for admission to the freshman class. He was not yet fourteen. But President Young was not the man to hold back a boy of quick mind and retentive memory, particularly when that boy was his "smart and amiable" young brother-in-law.

The entire course of study upon which John embarked was prescribed. A solid half of his time in class during the next four years was devoted to Latin and Greek classics; about a fourth, to mathematics and its applications. His remaining courses were brief introductions—no more than a term apiece—to rhetoric, logic, evidences of Christianity, mental philosophy, moral philosophy, astronomy, geology, chemistry, Constitution of the United States and national law, with two terms of natural philosophy.

The curriculum at Centre—similar in content and purpose to that which John's Grandfather Smith had administered at Princeton a generation earlier—was designed for gentlemen. Most of its graduates expected to enter one of the learned professions in a society which loved to savor the spoken word and to evaluate the performance of a speaker in any of the three principal forms of oratory—pulpit, legal, or political. Hence the faculty conducted "a regular exercise in reading and declamation, once a week . . . through the whole course—the Senior and Junior classes delivering original speeches."

Still more useful in shaping the style and increasing the fluency of John and his fellows who aspired to distinction in the Christian ministry, in law, or in public affairs were the lengthy Friday night meetings of the two literary societies, the Chamberlain and Deinologian. Both societies admitted college and grammar school students and both maintained libraries for the use of their members. The earliest extant records of the Deinologian Society, dating from November, 1835, show John C. Breckinridge already a member. In its meetings he took his turn delivering orations for the criticism of his peers and—what was more important—debating assigned questions dealing with current issues in public affairs or with religious or educational polity.

Breckinridge was very much at home at Centre. Until Christmas, 1835, his youngest uncle, the Reverend William L. Breckinridge, taught Latin and Greek at the college. In John's senior year President Young, then only thirty-five, was the eldest of a faculty of five. All the students met the president at prayers each day in the small, bare chapel. Juniors and seniors attended his classes in logic, mental and moral philosophy, evidences of Christianity, and Constitution of the United States and national law. A memorial tribute by a member of the class of 1845 recalled that he was "often foremost in our most active sports." Not surprisingly the college of his day (1830–57) has been termed his "extended shadow." For John, who lived in his home and ate at his table, he was a second father as well as friend, teacher, and counselor.

And that was not all. From 1834 until 1853 Young doubled as pastor of the Presbyterian church in Danville. In a report to the college trustees summarizing his first ten years as president, he mentioned as a matter of major import the college's almost annual experience of religious revivals. During one of those revivals, in March, 1835, in company with sundry of his fellow students, John became a communicant member of the Danville church.

In 1857 a Memphis clergyman, considerably Breckinridge's senior at Centre, recalled Breckinridge "as the sprightly and sportive boy of the preparatory and the Campus." The existence of the grammar school as an integral part of the college made for a wide range of ages within the college community. One of Breckinridge's early intimates at Centre was a boy named William Birney, son of abolitionist James G. Birney, who had once roomed at Princeton with John's father. Twenty years later, in spite of a wide divergence in their position on slavery, William recalled his boyhood days with John and wrote, "I feel the same affection for you that I did for the blue-eyed boy who read novels with me."

At Centre John also made firm friends of his first two law partners, the brothers Thomas and Samuel Bullock, and of an engaging Floridian, Charles C. Parkhill, who would one day marry his sister Laetitia.[3] Here too he met Beriah Magoffin, class of 1835, a political ally of later years, and Jeremiah T. Boyle, who would fight on the Union side in the Civil War. An otherwise unknown Deinologian of the class of 1841 wrote from Mississippi in December of that year that on receiving a letter from John, "joy inexpressible filled my heart . . . because a letter with your name recalled instantaneously a thousand schoolday moments more joyously spent with you."

When John received his bachelor's degree at the age of seventeen years and eight months, his future career was by no means settled. As his eldest Breckinridge uncle, John, wrote the next senior uncle, Robert, in Baltimore, "If he begins his profession *now,* he will be a *lawyer. . . . All his Kentucky friends,* . . . (& I agree with them) think he is too young to choose. He wishes to spend a year somewhere in reading history &c." This desire Uncle John approved. After mentioning various alternatives, he suggested that John might carry out his reading program as "a resident graduate" at Princeton. There, he thought, the young man would most likely be moved to follow his uncles and his maternal forebears into the ministry. As a token of his concern for a penniless nephew, Uncle John promised to subsidize him at the rate of $150 a year and urged his brother, who readily agreed, to do likewise. Before the end of October, young John started for Robert's manse, not alone but as the escort for "Grandma Black-Cap," who proposed to spend the winter in Baltimore, and for her sister, "Aunt Lewis," (born Elizabeth Cabell, the widow of Virginia Congressman William J. Lewis), who wished to return to Mt. Athos, her home near Lynchburg.

John spent much of the winter of 1838–39 as one of seven resident graduates at Princeton, where he lived in the home of his mother's niece, Theodosia Prevost. Thereafter he enjoyed his Uncle Robert's hospitality in Baltimore and accompanied him on a trip to New York City. He devoted the better part of the next summer to escorting his grandmother to her sister's home and then, with a hired wagon driver, taking the old ladies and their maids all the way back to Cabell's Dale. The two trips, eastward in 1838 and westward in 1839, introduced John to much of the Virginia countryside which he would be called on to defend in 1864.

Though his sweet-tempered great-aunt thought the young man a completely satisfactory escort, his rather demanding grandmother, while acknowledging that he had done the best he could, complained that he was "of little force." She added that he had left his boots at one Virginia tavern, his great coat at another. In fact, she exploded, "I was so mad I told him if he was not all in one piece he would leave a part of himself."

That autumn the object of the matriarch's wrath settled at Frankfort in the home of his sister Caroline and her husband, the Reverend Joseph J. Bullock, and began to read law under the direction of Judge William Owsley. As usual in a new situation, he found among his contemporaries in Frankfort new friends and boon companions. Notable among them were Theodore O'Hara, a dynamic fellow student of Judge Owsley, and Thomas L. Crittenden, then completing his legal studies under his father, Sen. John J. Crittenden.

During the summer of 1840 Breckinridge continued his studies at Cabell's Dale; in November he took a room in Lexington and enrolled in the second year of the law class at Transylvania University. There he studied under Chief Justice George Robertson and Judge Thomas A. Marshall of the Kentucky Court of Appeals and A. K. Woolley, a prominent Lexington attorney. On February 25, 1841, he received the bachelor of laws degree. The next day Robertson and Marshall licensed him to practice law in Kentucky.

Breckinridge's admission to the bar required him to decide where he should begin practice. While seeking advice and making up his mind, he performed a variety of legal chores for his Uncle Robert, delivered a Fourth of July oration at Frankfort, and stood by while his Uncle John died of tuberculosis at Cabell's Dale. Finally in October he and his friend Thomas W. Bullock, another Fayette County resident newly admitted to the bar, joined forces and set out on horseback to locate a frontier community which would provide a good prospect for the success of their partnership. They liked the soil and terrain in southeastern Iowa. After nearly three weeks of travel and reconnaissance, they decided that Burlington, county seat of Des Moines County and a Mississippi River port some sixty miles above the Missouri line, was the most promising spot in the territory for a pair of fledgling lawyers. They estimated the population of Burlington at two thousand and noted that it was growing rapidly.

In any event the town was crowded, and living quarters and office space were accordingly expensive. But the partners had anticipated some hardships and they took satisfaction, as healthy young men will, in enduring and reporting them. When John wrote that the firm of Breckinridge and Bullock proposed to sleep during the winter months on a straw mattress, Aunt Daphne, one of the household servants of the Bullock family, was astonished almost beyond belief "that one of old Waller Bullock's children" had come to such a pass. Breckinridge's mother, who had strongly objected to her son's leaving Kentucky, responded with some down-to-earth but earnest instructions about how a straw mattress might be padded to make it tolerably comfortable and warm. To cover it all, she urged the young man to procure a buffalo robe, which she had seen advertised in the Burlington newspaper which he sent her.

It was no complicated matter for the partners to hang up their shingle. District court, presided over by Charles Mason, chief justice of the territory, was in session when the young Kentuckians arrived. After a short examination, a committee of local lawyers recommended that they be admitted to practice in Iowa and they were sworn in forthwith. According to a notice which they presently inserted in a Burlington newspaper, they were prepared to practice in Des Moines County and a block of six other counties in southeastern Iowa, as well as in the Supreme Court of the territory, and to "act as General Agents for the purchase and sale of real estate."

As well prepared as most young lawyers of his time and early recognized as an eloquent advocate, Breckinridge could hardly have anticipated more professional success than came his way during his scant two years of practice in Burlington. In February, 1842, he predicted that he and his partner would make three or four hundred dollars that year and would earn enough in 1843 to support themselves. During the very cold winter of 1842–43, he reported that his firm ranked fourth or fifth among Burlington lawyers in number of suits in process during the current term of district court. And the records of the court sustain his claim.

Native intellectual capacity, personal integrity, the tact which enabled him to keep on good terms simultaneously with his mother and his Uncle Robert, eloquence long cultivated, and a winning personality were quite enough to build Breckinridge's reputation and to lay the foundation for outstanding professional success. He could not prosper greatly, however, for the times were hard. In August, 1842, Judge Mason signed uncontested decrees in bankruptcy for twenty-seven Des Moines County petitioners, whose liabilities ranged from $107 to $200,000. Here was an opportunity for the lawyers of the community, but Breckinridge and Bullock handled few bankruptcy cases. The young partners, like others in a similar situation, accepted produce of various kinds in payment of some fees. Many of their clients were very slow to pay.

When he moved to Iowa and for all of his life thereafter, Breckinridge, in spite of his solid Presbyterian upbringing, was not an active member of any church. The Session of the Danville church in the spring of 1840 had suspended him from membership at his own request on the ground that he no longer felt worthy to continue as a communicant. Hardly two months after his arrival in Iowa, however, he asked his relatives who were pastors— two surviving uncles and two brothers-in-law—to take up a collection to aid the small Presbyterian congregation of Burlington in building a meetinghouse. Immediately after his twenty-first birthday, he petitioned successfully for membership in Desmoines [sic] Lodge, No. 41, Ancient York Masons. Throughout the rest of his stay in Burlington he was active in the lodge and in a successful move to organize a grand lodge for Iowa. In December, 1842, he was elected senior warden of Desmoines Lodge.

Just before he started for Iowa, Breckinridge had received an encouraging letter from John J. Crittenden, then attorney general of the United States. Years later Breckinridge recalled that the Whig leader had "predicted to my delight and astonishment, that he would one day welcome me as a member of Congress from the West." Soon his Iowa friends were making a similar prediction, but by that time Breckinridge had allied himself firmly with the Democratic party. Though he came from a Whiggish family and a Kentucky county which was reliably Whig in election after election, he had, by one account, been leaning to the Democracy even before he left his native state. His partnership with Tom Bullock boosted his inclination, for Tom and his brother Sam followed their father's steady devotion to the Democratic cause. When ex-President Van Buren visited Lexington in 1842, it was "old Mr. Bullock" who welcomed the Little Magician and rode into town with him.

Some of Breckinridge's kinfolk and friends thought that his new political stand repesented a shrewd decision to join what promised to be the dominant party in what must soon be a new state. Others professed to believe that with experience he would come to his senses and join the respectables of central Kentucky under the Whig banner. Perhaps the most interesting reaction came in a letter from John C. Young:

You have become loco-foco.[4] Do you know what your Uncle Wil$^{\underline{m}}$ said when your Mother asked him what he felt when he heard of that fact in your history? "I felt as I would have done if I had heard that my daughter had been dishonored." This I presume was rather a strong figure of speech on the part of your uncle, who, you know, is not always very delicate or careful of extreme accuracy in his choice of figures or phraseology.

For his own part Young admitted that one could do worse than support Van Buren. But he sent his youthful brother-in-law an elaborate discussion of the theory of democracy and strongly advised that he take an active part in politics only after he had established himself as an able lawyer and had made a thorough study of the "grand principles" of politics.

Without complying fully with his brother-in-law's admonition and without much concern for the judgment of his earthy though reverend uncle, young Breckinridge plunged into politics. He began contributing partisan editorials to Burlington's Democratic weekly, the *Iowa Territorial Gazette and Advertiser.* He spoke at Democratic rallies and in February, 1843, he was named a member of his party's committee for Des Moines County.

John C. Breckinridge as a young man, about 1845
*Courtesy of Mr. and Mrs. John M. Prewitt and
Louisiana State University Press*

In the late summer of 1842, Breckinridge looked after the business of the firm in Burlington while his partner visited relatives and friends in Kentucky. In 1843 it was Breckinridge's turn to visit the Bluegrass region while Bullock kept shop on the banks of the Mississippi. But Breckinridge's visit ended in his decision, deeply regretted by a host of Iowa friends, to dissolve the firm and return to Kentucky.

Breckinridge's summer visit was prolonged until nearly the end of September, at first because he was unwell for several weeks, and then by two momentous developments. Late in the summer he met, wooed, and became engaged to a petite young woman of charm and some financial means, Mary Cyrene Burch of Georgetown.[5] Tied closely to this decision was one to return to Kentucky as a law partner of Tom Bullock's brother Samuel. Samuel as senior partner—he was nearly four years older than John—was to maintain his office in Lexington, and Breckinridge, his in Scott County at Georgetown. After devoting a few weeks to settling his affairs in Burlington and to trying some cases in the October term of the district court, he left Iowa almost exactly two years after his arrival and was soon back in Kentucky. On December 12 he and Mary were wed.

Whatever his reasons for leaving Iowa, he left behind many warm friends. A brother attorney wrote, "I need not tell you . . . how much I miss you as a boon companion, at the bar and in our political meetings." Another correspondent summed up the feelings of many:

You speak of the strong attachment you entertain for Burlington and its citizens. I assure you that that attachment is felt for you by . . . very many of the people of this place. . . . You would be received with open arms and a brighter prospect than yours here (should you return) never gilded the private or political horizon of any individual in the Western World. *Do come.*

Mary Cyrene Breckinridge, painted in 1860 by B. F. Reinhart
Courtesy of Mrs. James Carson Breckinridge

But Breckinridge had made his decision. Having sampled life near the frontier of settlement, he came home to the older community of central Kentucky. The young Democrat who had lived in a free territory came home to make a career as a lawyer and political leader in a community dominated by slaveholders. The young practitioner who had been subsidized during his stay in Iowa by various relatives, including his Uncle Robert, his cousin Theodosia Prevost, and his brother-in-law John C. Young, was now in a position to declare his financial independence.

Marriage to Mary Cyrene Burch brought her husband into a new circle of confusedly intermarried kinfolk based in Scott County—Burches, of course, Vileys (her mother's family), Johnsons, McConnells, Williamses, and the wealthy house of Ward. Many of them owned plantations and slaves in Mississippi, Louisiana, or Arkansas, as well as in Kentucky. The in-laws brought Breckinridge professional business as well as new social contacts and political support.

After a few months of "boarding," the young couple purchased for $1,250 a home which, with significant alterations and additions, still stands at the southwest corner of Broadway and College streets in Georgetown. But the business of the firm of Bullock and Breckinridge, particularly its Lexington business, grew so rapidly that the senior partner in July, 1845, urged that the junior's aid was needed in the Lexington office. It took little to persuade him. Within a month he sold the Georgetown house for $1,500, and the partners joined forces on North Upper Street, in the shadow of the Lexington courthouse. To conserve the Scott County business, Breckinridge announced that he would be in Georgetown for the monthly sessions of the County Court and for all terms of the Circuit Court.

John and Mary's first son, named Joseph Cabell for his paternal grandfather, had been born in the Georgetown home in December, 1844. In giving birth the young mother had suffered an extraordinarily painful labor, which nearly took her own life. For her husband, who had lost two sisters in childbirth, it was a shaking experience. A second son, called Clifton Rodes for his maternal grandfather, was born on November 22, 1846, in a more pretentious establishment on the edge of Lexington. In July of that year the expectant father had paid Jacob and Sarah Ashton $4,500 for some nineteen acres of land, including a much admired house of irregular shape, approached from South Broadway through a long, tree-bordered lane. The family continued to grow. A daughter, Frances (Fannie), was born in June, 1848, while Breckinridge was on his way home from military duty in Mexico, and a third son, John Milton, followed in August, 1849.

In the larger Breckinridge clan John was becoming a person of consequence. He was consulted on legal matters by his uncles and even by his Grandmother Breckinridge, who had once been infuriated by his youthful fecklessness. That lady, now blind, was still the vigorous head of her household and indeed of the entire family. She called John and his Uncle William into consultation in November, 1845, concerning the future of a wayward, spendthrift cousin, Samuel M. Breckinridge, aged seventeen, the only son of the Reverend John Breckinridge. The upshot of the family council was that grandmother agreed to pay Sam's expenses for the winter of 1845–46 at Mrs. Dunham's, where John, newly transferred to Lexington, was boarding. Sam in turn promised to behave himself and to begin at once to read law under John's direction.

In politics the young lawyer was laying foundations. When Sam Breckinridge arrived in Kentucky during the electoral campaign of 1844, he heard before he had seen John that he was "making himself very conspicuous here by making flaming Loco-foco speeches at the Barbecues." Already John was in demand as a fluent speaker, familiar with the issues of the campaign and ready to debate with Whig opponents ranging from men of his own age to ex-Governor Thomas Metcalfe. In 1845 he took the stump for Dr. A. K. Marshall, Democratic candidate for Congress in the Eighth District, which included Fayette and Scott counties. In 1847, with numerous other Democrats and some Whigs, he for a time urged the election of General Zachary Taylor as president without reference to party. But in 1848, when Taylor had accepted a Whig nomination, Breckinridge supported the Democratic nominees, Lewis Cass of Michigan, and his late commanding general, William O. Butler of Carrollton, Kentucky.

The outbreak of the Mexican War in 1846 had led Breckinridge to apply for a place on Butler's staff. He had known the older man, a veteran of the War of 1812, at least since Butler's unsuccessful campaign as the Democratic nominee for governor in 1844. Butler replied that the members of a general officer's staff had by law to be taken from "officers of the line." Since Breckinridge did not have a commission as a line officer, the best Butler could do was to offer him a place as an unsalaried volunteer aide and to advise against his accepting it.

Two volunteer regiments of infantry and one of cavalry, enlisted in Kentucky for twelve months' service, fought in northern Mexico during the first year of the war. The First Infantry had a galling defensive assignment at Monterey, where General Butler was wounded; the Second Kentucky Infantry and the First Kentucky Cavalry both suffered heavy casualties at the Battle of Buena Vista. Though the Kentucky troops had fought well, the survivors were glad to return to Kentucky at the expiration of their term of enlistment. On July 20, 1847, many of them, with thousands of their fellow citizens, assembled at Frankfort for the solemn reinterment of the bodies of Col. William H. McKee and Lt. Col. Henry Clay, Jr., of the Second Kentucky Infantry, Lt. Edward M. Vaughan, adjutant of the First Kentucky Cavalry (Breckinridge's fellow student in the Transylvania law class six years earlier), and fourteen other officers and enlisted men. Breckinridge had been selected to give the funeral oration. Fulfilling the assignment "in an eloquent and impressive style," he is thought by some to have impressed himself as well as the audience. In any event, when Governor Owsley on August 31 called for two more Kentucky Infantry regiments "to serve for the duration of the war," the orator at once applied for a commission in one of the new units. At the time General Scott's campaign for Mexico City had not yet been brought to a successful conclusion; neither Breckinridge nor Owsley could know that the serious fighting would be over before the new regiments could be mustered in.

Though the governor had directed the first stage of Breckinridge's legal studies, he was a Whig. So the would-be officer, through his friend Tom Crittenden, enlisted the influence of Crittenden's father, who was again representing Kentucky in the United States Senate. The governor quickly decided that one of the field officers of the new Third Regiment should be drawn from the ranks of the Democracy. Thus, selecting Whigs Manlius V. Thomson, a Georgetown lawyer, and young Crittenden as colonel and lieutenant colonel respectively, he offered Breckinridge a commission as major on September 4. Crittenden had served through the 1846–47 campaign in northern Mexico as a volunteer aide on the staff of General Taylor. Thomson had been lieutenant governor from 1840 until 1844, but like Breckinridge he had no previous military experience.

The rush to enlist was impressive. Some companies had to be rejected and in the end Thomson's regiment of a thousand men consisted of ten companies, one each enrolled in Laurel, Estill, Bath, Fleming, Nicholas, Boone, Shelby, Scott, Bourbon, and Fayette counties. The Fourth Regiment, under Col. John S. Williams, who had distinguished himself at the Battle of Cerro Gordo in May, and Lt. Col. William Preston, included companies from ten more counties. Early in October the two Kentucky regiments were mustered into service and went into training, seven miles downriver from Louisville. On November 1 they paraded through Louisville and embarked on river steamboats. Six days later they reached New Orleans. By November 21, with three other regiments assigned to General Butler's command, they had landed at Vera Cruz.

Camped in the pestilential lowland nearby, the troops took sick in droves. Butler accordingly hurried to move his men into the highlands. Leaving Vera Cruz on November 27 and following for the most part the partly broken paved road constructed in Cortés's time, the two Kentucky regiments reached Mexico City on December 18, after two-day stops at Jalapa and Puebla. Blistered feet, sickness, bitterly cold nights, and a shortage of bacon and coffee made the march a hardship for the green troops. Many sick men were left in a hospital established at Jalapa. There were, however, no hostilities during the 253-mile trek, though the men were put in combat formation once or twice because of false reports of danger from bands of Mexican guerrillas. Major Breckinridge won friends among the men of his regiment by giving up his horse to a succession of sick and footsore soldiers. One admiring report indicates that he actually rode less than two of the eighteen days of the march.

In Mexico City the enlisted men of the Third Regiment were quartered in two convents from which the nuns had been evacuated. The men found the city as peaceable as Louisville, according to a lieutenant who reported to the *Louisville Journal* late in December. So they settled down to occupation duty while the peace treaty was negotiated and signed, dispatched to Washington, reluctantly accepted by President Polk, approved by the Senate, and returned to Mexico for action by the Mexican Congress. Finally on May 30, 1848, the formal exchange of ratifications took place. On that day General Butler, who had succeeded Scott in the chief command on February 18, began moving his troops toward Vera Cruz.

During his six months in Mexico City, Breckinridge

took his turn in the routine assignments of a field grade officer. On one occasion, with Colonel Thomson and Capt. Leander M. Cox of the Third Kentucky, he was a supper guest of General Scott himself. A soldier later recalled playing ball with Breckinridge against the wall of one of the convents occupied by the regiment. Another enlisted man remembered having spent several evenings with him in a Masonic lodge which met in Thomson's quarters. Soldiers and at least one American civilian who fell afoul of martial law sought his professional aid. During the Court of Inquiry which sat in Mexico City from March 16 until April 22 to investigate the conduct of Brig. Gen. Gideon J. Pillow, against whom Scott had preferred charges, Breckinridge served as one of Pillow's counsel. But the official record shows that Pillow conducted his own case, once he had introduced Breckinridge and another officer as his assistant counsel.

Retracing its steps to the coast, the Third Regiment embarked at Vera Cruz on June 29. Following a short delay at New Orleans, it reached Louisville on July 16. Thousands of Kentuckians turned out to give the troops a hearty welcome home. The men were mustered out as quickly as possible; by nightfall on July 21 the young major was again a civilian. In a scant ten months he had of necessity become acquainted with the fundamentals of military discipline, regimental drill, and administration. He had broadened his acquaintance and his stature with the men of the two Kentucky regiments. He may have studied strategy and tactics, but there is no direct evidence that he did. Certainly he had no combat experience. But he had acquired a military title and would be addressed as Major Breckinridge until he attained higher military rank in a much more significant conflict.

2

RISING PARTY LEADER

B Y HIS TWENTY-EIGHTH birthday on January 16, 1849, Breckinridge had come a long way. In the five years since his marriage and return to Kentucky, he had gained recognition as a lawyer of integrity and skill. His eloquence, already much admired, had contributed greatly to his success at the bar and to his position as a leader of his party in central Kentucky. With a devoted wife and three young children he occupied an "elegant mansion," set amid spacious grounds on the outskirts of Lexington. Through military service he had won many new friends and admirers.

Now his career took a sharp turn. For the first time he became a candidate for elective office. And faced with an issue which was to trouble the nation for the next sixteen years, he put himself squarely on record as strongly proslavery. Nominated by a bipartisan mass meeting called to guard the interests of Kentucky slaveholders, the young Democrat won a seat in the legislature as a representative of his native county, still a Whig stronghold.

After a single term in the Kentucky House of Representatives, Breckinridge took a much greater plunge in 1851 when he sought election to the federal Congress as the representative of Henry Clay's own Ashland district. His victory over Leslie Combs, a longtime intimate of the great Whig leader, was a startling upset. Two years later he won reelection by defeating "Black Bob" Letcher, ex-congressman, ex-governor, ex-minister to Mexico, and one of the most astute vote-getters in the Whig ranks.

These electoral triumphs thrilled Democrats and earned the youthful victor a national reputation. Even in his first term he gained recognition as an effective spokesman for his party in the House of Representatives. In his second term he played an important role in shaping and passing the fateful Kansas-Nebraska Bill. He became influential in the administration of President Pierce, who offered him the governorship of Washington Territory in 1853, nominated him as minister to Spain two years later, and would have made him governor of Minnesota had he found an adequate excuse for removing the incumbent.

Meanwhile Breckinridge had become acquainted with almost everyone of consequence in national politics. He had become an intimate of fellow Democrats Stephen A. Douglas, the Little Giant from Illinois, and Douglas's rival, Sen. Jesse D. Bright of Indiana. The wealthy Washington banker, W. W. Corcoran, had contributed generously to his campaign chest when he ran for reelection in 1853 and had backed his investment in Superior City at the northwestern corner of Wisconsin. In 1851 Lazarus W. Powell of Henderson, one of Breckinridge's personal and political friends, became the first Democrat to win the governorship of Kentucky since 1832. In political alliance with Powell and James Guthrie of Louisville, Pierce's secretary of the treasury, Breckinridge was already one of the most potent leaders among Kentucky Democrats when in 1855 he firmly refused to run for a third term in Congress. Meanwhile too his wife had borne three more children, one of them lost in infancy.

When the young man decided against a third race for Congress, he acted ostensibly on the view that his obligations to his growing family required him to seek fortune at the expense of fame. No longer an office holder or office seeker, he could devote nearly all his time to an increasingly lucrative legal practice. And he would be in a better position to extend the land purchases in the West which were his investment in the future of his country for the future of his children.

In his first political candidacy Breckinridge took a position sharply opposed to that of his brother-in-law and mentor, John C. Young, and his uncles, Robert and William Breckinridge. The situation calls for some explanation. In 1848 Kentucky voters had authorized a convention to revise the Constitution of 1799. The legislature set the meeting for October, 1849; delegates were to be chosen at the general election, August 6–8. Long before the voters and the legislature acted, however, it was apparent that the future of slavery in Kentucky would be a major issue at the convention.

Early in 1849 John's two uncles and brother-in-law and the impetuous Cassius M. Clay came forward to organize the "friends of emancipation" in preparation for the convention. On April 25 they were among the conspicuous leaders in an *ad hoc* convention at Frankfort which proposed to run "friends of emancipation" in every county as candidates for the constitutional convention. Those candidates would be pledged to support "the complete power in the people of Kentucky to enforce and perfect in or under the new Constitution, a system of gradual, prospective emancipation of slaves," and to include in the Constitution "the absolute prohibition of the importation of any more slaves into Kentucky." In May, Robert Breckinridge, since 1847 pastor of the First Presbyterian Church in Lexington, accepted a nomination of the "friends of emancipation" for one of Fayette County's seats in the convention.[1]

The moderate character of the preacher's platform was indicated by a further resolution of the April convention that "every scheme for the compulsory extinction of slavery in Kentucky ought to begin with those born after the commencement of the scheme, and that the removal of the liberated slaves ought to form a part of every such plan."

In a hotly defensive response to this mildest possible form of emancipation, the unswerving proslavery men in turn organized to gain control of the convention and the next legislature. At the end of May, responding to a public letter asking his views, John Breckinridge made his position clear. In the local newspapers he published a reply indicating his opposition to "impairing in any form" the existing constitutional provisions recognizing and protecting the institution of slavery. Accordingly he opposed emancipation and any general law prohibiting the importation of slaves into the state. He was willing, however, to support legislation (such a measure was already on the statute book) prohibiting the importation of "slaves as merchandise." He believed "that indiscriminate importation would have the effect of depreciating the character and value of our slave population."

On June 11 a bipartisan, proslavery mass meeting in Fayette County named John C. Breckinridge (Democrat) and Dr. D. L. Price (Whig) to seek the county's two seats in the state house of representatives and Oliver Anderson (Whig) to run for the state senate. It also ratified the earlier selection of Judge A. K. Woolley (Whig) and Robert Nelson Wickliffe (Democrat) as candidates for election to the convention. The same day a meeting of regular Whigs nominated Robert S. Todd, father-in-law of Abraham Lincoln, for the state senate and Dr. Richard J. Spurr and attorney Henry C. Pindell for the state house of representatives. The Democrats as such made no nomination in the county.

The subsequent eight-week canvass was most unusual. Newspapers which reported both the Whig nominations and those of the bipartisan, proslavery meeting also reported the first 1849 cases of cholera in the city of Lexington. The much-feared malady had been epidemic earlier at the State Lunatic Asylum in the city's outskirts, but now it spread through city and countryside. Though several of the nominees suffered attacks, both Breckinridges were spared. Woolley, who had earlier been reported cured, died three days before the election. In the midst of campaigning John Breckinridge lost his law partner. Samuel Bullock, two of whose slaves had already died, was taken violently ill on the morning of July 12 and died that evening at his home near Walnut Hill, five miles southeast of Lexington. In spite of the spreading epidemic, many of the usual barbecues and other political meetings took place. And John, with other candidates for convention and legislature, carried his message to the voters who had the courage to attend.

The election days came before the epidemic had run its course in Fayette County. Uncle and nephew, true to their principles, voted against each other. The younger Breckinridge polled 1,481 votes against 1,024 for Pindell and 913 for Price. Since the county was entitled to two representatives, both Breckinridge and Pindell won seats. The proslavery nominees for convention and senate were all elected, though the death of Woolley had required a hurried substitution in his place. Except for Breckinridge, no Fayette candidate for convention or legislature polled more votes than Pindell, who had made it clear that he too opposed emancipation in any form. John's margin of victory is particularly impressive when one remembers that Price, nominated with him by the proslavery mass meeting, ran third, with 568 fewer votes than his running mate.[2]

Breckinridge was a busy man during the interval between the August election and the convening of the legislature on the last day of the year. Almost at once he formed a new partnership with George B. Kinkead, a man nearly ten years his senior and a Whig who had served briefly as secretary of state under Governor Owsley. In September Breckinridge and thirty-seven other Democrats joined to establish a Democratic newspaper, the *Kentucky Statesman,* to be published semiweekly at

Lexington. The new paper began publication in October. As Breckinridge moved into national politics, the *Statesman* would often be referred to as his personal organ. Just before the legislature met he had the sad duty of arranging the funeral of his college mate, Charles C. Parkhill, the much-loved husband of his sister Laetitia.

The legislative session lasted hardly two weeks longer than the electoral campaign. At the opening of the session Breckinridge's fellow Democrats gave him the compliment of their votes for Speaker of the House of Representatives on the first three of seven ballots. In the end the Whigs, with three-fifths of the membership, united to elect one of their number. But Breckinridge, as a colleague reported three years later, "was emphatically the *leader* of the Democracy in that General Assembly." Most of the measures adopted were local or personal, however, and in any case petty.

Far overshadowing such matters were the broader issues with which the legislators at Washington wrestled during the prolonged session of the Thirty-first Congress, beginning in December, 1849, and adjourning only in September, 1850. In that session all the bitterness stirred up by the need to settle the future of slavery in the territories acquired through the Mexican War came to a head. Ominous threats of secession, should Congress adopt a solution considered unfair to the South, were openly voiced on the floor of both houses. On January 29 Kentucky's venerable Henry Clay proposed to the Senate a series of measures by which he hoped to reach a settlement and which indeed provided a basis for the Union-saving Compromise of 1850, adopted finally in September.

In his message at the opening of the General Assembly, Gov. J. J. Crittenden had alluded to the excitement in Congress and the country and had preached a brief, sound homily on the value of the Union to all its members and particularly to Kentucky. Moved by the seriousness of the situation, Breckinridge and other legislators offered resolutions purporting to state Kentucky's views on the issues at stake. All these resolutions were referred to the Committee on Federal Relations, of which Breckinridge, two other Democrats, and four Whigs were members.

On February 7 the Whig majority of the committee reported a set of resolutions which, among other things, endorsed Clay's proposals, "as a fair, equitable and just *basis* upon which this exciting and dangerous question may be settled," and asked the Kentucky delegation in Congress "to carry out our wishes, herein expressed, and make the preservation of the Union and its peace, the paramount object of their exertions." Breckinridge, for the Democratic minority, offered an alternative set of resolutions. He urged that it was preferable to that of the majority because it clearly denied that Congress had the power "to interfere with the institution of slavery either in the States, . . . the District of Columbia, or the Territories." The majority report, on the other hand, only urged Congress to refrain from legislating on slavery in the District or the Territories, thus possibly conceding that Congress might actually have the power to do so. Breckinridge's minority report also called explicitly for a stronger fugitive slave law than that of 1793.

Near the close of the session the House voted to lay on the table the report of its own committee and also the resolutions on the subject, previously adopted by the Senate. Breckinridge had failed to get his minority report adopted, but neither had the House adopted the milder, though still proslavery, version proposed by the majority of the committee or that adopted by the Senate. For the rest of his career in politics, Breckinridge would not move far from the position on slavery in Kentucky which he took in 1849 and that on slavery in the country at large, particularly in the territories, which he adopted in 1850.[3]

Though Breckinridge had taken positive ground as a spokesman for the proslavery majority in Kentucky, he was by no means a large slaveholder. The census of 1850 showed him the owner of two black women, aged thirty-six and twenty, a mulatto man of twenty-three, a boy of fourteen, and a girl of eleven. Meanwhile he had expanded his homestead by purchase to 26½ acres worth $7,000.

Shortly before the legislature adjourned, Breckinridge joined sixty-four of his colleagues in forming a bipartisan organization to work for the adoption of the proposed new constitution—"the People's Constitution," as the *Kentucky Statesman* dubbed it. Throughout the legislative session, however, he had been distressed by illness in his immediate family. On March 18 Baby Johnny, less than a year old, died. The bereaved father cancelled an engagement to speak that night at Georgetown on behalf of the new constitution; but he subsequently fulfilled similar engagements there, at Lexington, and elsewhere in the vicinity. When the referendum was taken, May 6–7, 1850, he had the satisfaction of knowing that 77 percent of the voters—a majority in every county except one—favored the new fundamental law. As Breckinridge had urged, that document gave no comfort to those who sought the emancipation of Kentucky's slaves, even at some distant date. In approved Democratic fashion it provided that all judges should henceforth be elected by the voters, not appointed by the governor as under the old constitution. It also replaced the old, virtually self-perpetuating county courts with new ones whose members, as well as other county officers, would be popularly elected for limited terms.

Breckinridge declined to seek a second term in the legislature. He had sacrificed professional business to make the previous year's canvass; now he said that "considerations of a private but imperative character" would keep him from becoming a candidate. He had reason enough. His wife, sorrowing at the loss of her little son, was pregnant again; in December she bore her fifth child, John Witherspoon.

Meanwhile Breckinridge seized an opportunity to widen his political base. In October, as a member of the Committee on Resolutions and Toasts, he helped plan an immense bipartisan Union festival and barbecue held near Lexington to celebrate the passage of the Compromise of 1850 and particularly to honor Kentucky's venerable Senator Clay for his leadership in bringing it about. The assembled crowd adopted resolutions which endorsed the compromise and thanked God and the members of Congress who had helped adopt it for arresting "the dissolution of the Union" and averting a ruinous civil war. Members of the committee offered ten toasts. Breckinridge, now a recognized spokesman of the Democratic party, proposed one to the great Whig leader:

HENRY CLAY—Kentucky, with one heart and one voice, places Henry Clay where, during the late session of Congress, he had placed himself, *high above the platform of party,* and on this lofty eminence she proudly presents him for the admiration of the present and coming ages. This priceless honor is the gift not of party, but of his country, for his spirit[ed] stirring eloquence, his lofty patriotism and courage in defence of our beloved Union, the last hope of freedom and of mankind. Nobly has he won the honor—long may he wear it.

In responding to Breckinridge's toast Clay

spoke of Maj. B. in terms of strong personal regard and esteem. He said that he was happy to unite on such an occasion, with the son and grandson of his old friends; and after complimenting Maj. B. upon his talents and standing, expressed the hope and belief that he would employ both for the benefit of his country.[4]

The old senator's remarks were often interpreted by Breckinridge's admirers as a solemn political blessing of the young speaker and certainly did him no harm.

But party politics had not been abandoned; and January 8, 1851, the anniversary of Jackson's victory at New Orleans, found Breckinridge taking a prominent part in the Democratic state convention at Frankfort, which nominated Powell for governor. Then on the eve of his thirtieth birthday the *Kentucky Statesman* announced that the major had agreed to be a candidate for Congress in the Eighth District. Widely known as the Ashland district, this constituency took its name from Clay's estate. It included Fayette, Jessamine, Bourbon, Woodford, Franklin, Scott, and Owen counties. Breckinridge's candidacy was an act of faith in himself, for the Whig majority in the district was conservatively estimated at from 600 to 1,000 votes. The Democrats had not even contested the previous election.

The campaign was long and grueling. As early as February 10, Breckinridge spoke for over an hour to a large audience at the Lexington courthouse. Like the grandfather whom he had never seen, he emphasized as fundamental "the doctrine of a strict construction of the constitution." Bringing the issue up to date, he saw it particularly as a weapon against the exercise by Congress of "unlimited dominion over the territories, excluding the people of the slave states from emigrating thither with their property." In an eloquent tribute to the Union, he made it clear that he spoke of *"a union . . . under the Constitution,* which defines its own powers and prohibits aggression upon the rights of the citizen and the sovereignty of the States." Thus at the beginning of his first candidacy for Congress the orator stated the basic principles—strict construction and a central government of limited powers—upon which he would stand throughout his career in national affairs. He valued strict construction not merely for its own sake or solely as a means of limiting the general power of the central government. He thought it especially valuable as a tool to keep Congress from prohibiting slavery in the territories.

Early in April, Combs and Breckinridge met at Frankfort in debate. In May, conforming to the custom of the day, they began a joint canvass of the district. Devoting a week or more to each county, they met day after day at 1:30 or 2 P.M. at a different village, crossroads, mill, or grove. Chatting, listening, telling stories, and shaking hands with the "sovereigns" before the speaking began, Breckinridge won the heart of many a semiliterate yeoman. He also proved a more effective debater than his competitor, a man nearly twice his age. His victory thrilled Democrats throughout the country. Combs carried the richer Bluegrass counties—Bourbon, Fayette, Woodford, and Jessamine—by margins ranging from 354 to 11 votes. But Breckinridge carried Franklin County by 34 votes, Scott by 508, and hardscrabble Owen by 677. Of a total of 10,808 votes, he received approximately 52½ percent. At the same time Powell won the governorship by a tiny plurality of 850 votes in a total poll of over 111,000. The 3,621 votes won by a third candidate, emancipationist Cassius Clay, are enough to explain Powell's margin of victory. But the Democrats, who had won the governorship for the first time since 1832 and elected five of the state's ten congressmen, were elated.

Breckinridge's campaign for reelection in 1853 followed the same pattern as his first congressional race, except for two things. Regardless of cost the Whigs were determined to recover his seat, which they had come to consider rightfully theirs. They poured money into the district; in response Breckinridge's friends in New York, Washington, and Louisville rallied to help his constituents furnish his campaign chest. And the wily former governor Robert P. Letcher, who had won fourteen popular elections and lost none, was a more dangerous opponent than Combs. He was almost exactly twice the age of his young rival.

In this campaign Breckinridge found an unlikely ally in Cassius Clay. An old enemy of Letcher from the days when both Clay and Letcher were Whigs, Clay now played the role of spoiler. "In pursuance of my policy of disruption," he wrote in his memoirs a generation later,

"I, of course, sided with Breckinridge—not as a Democrat, but the opponent of Letcher and Whigery [sic]." Speaking of a debate between Breckinridge and Letcher near the edge of Fayette County, close to Clay's home base in Madison County, Clay continued:

The contrast between the men was itself an argument. Breckinridge was tall, well-formed, with . . . regular face of great mental power . . . , intellectual, composed, and full of conscious genius and future prowess. Letcher . . . had grown so corpulent . . . that he seemed at times on the very verge of suffocation or apoplexy. The weather was very warm. Breckinridge went at him with the coolness of a skilled swordsman; making home-thrusts, and coolly observing the effect of each. Letcher was very much confused, greatly angry, and fought as one who had lost . . . even eye-sight. The perspiration poured off him; and he literally "larded the earth." His voice was guttural, and ejected from his lungs as a badly-charged fuse of wet and dry powder.

When election day came after a campaign of three and a half months, 12,538 votes were recorded, 1,730 more than in 1851. Breckinridge's margin of victory, 526 votes, was almost identical with his earlier margin over Combs. Again an overwhelming victory in Scott and Owen counties overcame the Whig lead in the richer counties of the inner Bluegrass. Owen County had long been reliably Democratic, but it outdid itself this time. Its total vote exceeded by 123 the number of adult male freemen on the county assessor's books, and Breckinridge ran off with 71 percent of the votes polled. In jocular but genuine appreciation, family and friends began calling the congressman's youngest son "Owen County." Soon the nickname was mercifully shortened to Owen, and thus the boy was known until adulthood. For Breckinridge and his supporters the ever-faithful county was thenceforth "Sweet Owen."

In both his congressional races Breckinridge received the support of some Whigs. When Letcher in 1853 argued that Henry Clay's old district ought to be represented by a Whig, Breckinridge in reply could speak truthfully of his own friendly relations with the old statesman. After his first election to Congress he paid a call of respect at Ashland. During the ten months which remained before Clay's death, he cultivated the relationship. Without in any way compromising his party principles, he made no secret of his belief that Clay was one of the great men of his generation. When Breckinridge returned to Washington in May, 1852, after a short visit in Kentucky, he carried a rose which Clay's wife had sent the dying senator from his own garden. A daily visitor during the old man's final weeks, he listened while Clay spoke "of his family, his friends, and his country," and finally of his religious faith. After the end came, the young Democrat rose in the House to pay a moving tribute to the fallen leader. He praised him above all for his "genuine and enlarged patriotism" in a succession of crises "threatening the existence of the Union." He recalled particularly the crisis of 1849–50:

It is fresh in the memory of us all that, when lately the fury of sectional discord threatened to sever the Confederacy, Mr. Clay, though withdrawn from public life and oppressed by the burden of years, came back to the Senate, the theatre of his glory, and devoted the remnant of his strength to the sacred duty of preserving the union of the States.

Small wonder that many a Kentucky Whig and many a young man who might have become a Whig had Clay lived, turned instead to follow Breckinridge's rising star.

Breckinridge, like most members, did not ordinarily keep house in Washington. Rather, he rented bachelor quarters in one or another of the many rooming houses which catered to the needs, if not the comfort, of congressmen. During the winter of 1852–53, for instance, he lived in the home of Mrs. Peterson on Tenth Street, between E and F streets, the modest house in which Abraham Lincoln was to die a dozen years later. That session he belonged to a "mess" at the Irving Hotel on Pennsylvania Avenue, together with a senator from Delaware and one from Vermont, three representatives from Virginia and three from New England. When his wife, who gave birth, March 31, 1854, to the couple's last child, joined him in Washington early in June, he rented the home of a clergyman who was to be out of town for the summer. But wherever he slept or ate, Breckinridge, from the start of his service at the capital, always protected himself against monotony in diet and liquid refreshment not up to his standard by procuring adequate quantities of the best Kentucky bacon, ham, and whiskey.

During both of Breckinridge's terms as a congressman his party enjoyed a substantial majority in the House of Representatives; handsome, white-haired Linn Boyd, long the representative of the First District in the extreme western end of Kentucky, was elected Speaker. But during the Thirty-second Congress, as Breckinridge often reminded patronage-seeking constituents, the Whig administration of President Fillmore controlled the executive branch. In the Thirty-third Congress, with Pierce in the White House and Guthrie at the treasury, the young congressman was a figure of greater influence. The fact that only 80 of the 234 members of the House had served in the Thirty-second Congress enhanced the position of the eloquent and personable representative from central Kentucky.

Breckinridge's vigorous efforts to carry Kentucky for Pierce, though unsuccessful by some 3,200 votes in a total of 110,000, had earned him the recognition of the new administration. When he reached home in September, 1852, following the adjournment of Congress, less than two months remained before election day. With real dedication he threw himself into the campaign. He spoke almost daily, often for an hour and a half, in a succession of county seat towns in the Bluegrass and in the western fringe of the mountains of eastern Kentucky. By the first of October his calendar was so full that he had to decline further engagements. At Harrodsburg on October 5 the crowd was much too large to be accommodated in the courthouse. Standing in one of the windows, Breckinridge spoke simultaneously to those in the courtroom and those who had been unable to get inside. At Harrodsburg his friend, Beriah Magoffin, lent him a good riding horse to carry him from one appointment to the next. After about two weeks' service the horse, furloughed briefly for pasture and rest near Winchester, broke out and ran away. The election over and the horse still missing, Magoffin refused to worry about the loss. "I feel amply compensated in the services you have rendered the cause of democracy if you never get him," he wrote. Then, shifting in exultant tones to the party victory in the country as a whole, he added,

We may well be proud of the brilliant triumph we have won. . . . The desponding hopes of the South have been revived. . . . The slave states have the assurance that the sacred bonds of the Union cannot be broken—that the Constitution will be perpetual. . . . The North too has come gloriously to the rescue. . . .

Numerous Democrats shared Magoffin's optimistic enthusiasm about their party's victory and his gratitude for Breckinridge's strenuous campaigning. In the rush for rewards the campaigner for a time sought appointment as governor of Washington Territory; accordingly he solicited and received recommendations to the president-elect from Governor Powell and General Butler. Soon after the inauguration the offer of appointment came. By that time, however, Breckinridge, after consulting his wife and friends at home, had decided to decline the opportunity in the Pacific Northwest and to run for reelection to Congress.

Within the framework of broad public policy to which

he was committed, Breckinridge had made a good and consistent record. He had stood for governmental economy, particularly opposing appropriations for internal improvements. On the other hand he had made a strong and successful stand for a modest appropriation to keep the two government–owned bridges across the eastern branch of the Potomac in good repair, in order to avoid greater costs later on. On the ground that there was a surplus of junior naval officers, he had opposed an amendment to the naval appropriation bill which would have authorized the president to appoint ten additional midshipmen to the Naval Academy. He had catechized abolitionist Joshua R. Giddings on the floor of the House and arraigned him for his admitted intention of interposing every possible obstacle, legal and personal, in the way of owners seeking to recover fugitive slaves. Reflecting the artistic taste of many of his fellow citizens, he objected strongly to appropriating $50,000 to employ a popular sculptor to create a new statue of George Washington. He had no objection to the project, he said, if the Father of his Country were to appear in continental uniform; what he disliked was the fact that the sculptor proposed to show him in a Roman toga. Breckinridge also took a leading part in an unsuccessful effort to keep Congress from increasing its subsidy to the Collins line of steamships for carrying the transatlantic mail from New York to Liverpool and back. Indeed, it was alleged that the Collins interest, recognizing him as a dangerous enemy, provided some of the funds used to fight his reelection.

Breckinridge's maiden speech was a vigorous defense of Kentucky's favorite son, General Butler, his old commander and his personal preference for president in 1852, against a double-barreled attack. The first barrel was a speech by Whig Congressman E. C. Cabell of Florida, a distant cousin; the second was two blistering articles by a fellow Kentuckian, George N. Sanders, newly installed editor of the *Democratic Review*.

Speaking initially on March 4, Breckinridge effectively denied Cabell's charge that Butler was a "mum" candidate whose views on slavery were unknown and that, though he was a Southerner and a slaveholder, he was really in sympathy with the Free Soil wing of the Democratic party. On the contrary, Breckinridge showed that Butler was a man of firm convictions who had approved in advance the resolutions adopted on Jackson Day, 1852, by the state convention of Kentucky Democrats. Those resolutions, after first asserting the extreme proslavery view that slaveholders had a constitutional right to carry their human chattels into any of the territories of the United States and to hold them there in slavery, indicated a willingness to abide by the provisions of the 1850 compromise.[5]

Having disposed of Cabell, Breckinridge moved on to Sanders's attacks in the January and February issues of the *Review*. In a thinly veiled manner the first article had damned all the Democratic candidates for president, except Stephen A. Douglas, as "old fogies" without a program which would appeal to the progressive "Young America" element in the party. The February article denounced Butler by name. Defending his old commander and the Kentucky Democracy, Breckinridge insisted that Douglas must assume responsibility for Sanders's scurrilous attack. Shifting from personalities to principles, the young congressman took a characteristically conservative line. He feared that Sanders's "Young America" program would take the country far "beyond the limits of the Federal Constitution." The party, he urged, must "adhere with immovable fidelity to the ancient and distinguished land-marks of its policy."

Democratic newspapers all over the country reprinted the speech. Winning praise from every quarter, it brought the orator nationwide recognition. Charles L. Woodbury of Boston summed up the response: "Your speech has created much sensation. . . . I hear it continually spoken of as the best speech of the session." Breckinridge's Kentucky friends were particularly pleased and impressed. They thought that he had handled himself well and had defended Butler manfully. Butler, in the warmest possible terms, thanked him for his effort. As it developed, however, the general's endorsement of the Kentucky convention's resolutions—clearly avowed in a letter to the venerable Jacksonian, Francis P. Blair, which Breckinridge had read aloud during his speech—ended any chance that his candidacy would attract significant support in the northern wing of the party and effectively killed what little prospect he had of nomination.

During Breckinridge's second term the fires of the slavery controversy, supposedly dampened by the adoption of the Compromise of 1850, flared up unexpectedly in the four-month debate which preceded the enactment in May, 1854, of a bill for organizing the Kansas and Nebraska territories. This is not the place to discuss the motives which led Senator Douglas to report a bill for organizing as Nebraska territory the entire region from Missouri and the Missouri River to the Rockies and from the parallel of 36°30′ to that of 49°.[6] Nor is it necessary to explain here why the bill, as amended, debated, and adopted under Douglas's leadership, provided for two territories and declared the Missouri Compromise prohibition of slavery in this area

inoperative and void; it being the true intent and meaning of this act not to legislate slavery into any Territory or State, nor to exclude it therefrom, but to leave the people thereof perfectly free to form and regulate their domestic institutions in their own way, subject only to the Constitution of the United States.[7]

When Congressman Breckinridge's formidable Uncle Robert wrote him in sharp criticism of the bill, the younger man assumed responsibility for it. Courteously but proudly he asserted that he "had more to do than any other man here, in putting it in its present shape." As to his initiative in the matter, we have only his own testimony. But it is a fact that he was one of the several Democratic members of the two houses who conferred with President Pierce, Sunday, January 22, and persuaded him to accept the general principle that the Missouri Compromise prohibition should be set aside and to draft the first version of the critical section which declared it "inoperative."

In his principal speech for the bill on the floor of the House of Representatives on March 23, Breckinridge dealt with a major objection—namely, that the elimination of the congressional prohibition of slavery violated a pledge of good faith, a compact almost as solemn as the Constitution itself. He argued that the Missouri Compromise of 1820 had been violated the very next year by northern congressmen who refused to admit Missouri without a further "compromise and condition." Further, he claimed that the northern opponents of the Kansas-Nebraska Bill consistently refused to apply the principles of the Missouri Compromise to the territory acquired from Mexico. Instead they had demanded that Congress prohibit slavery in all that territory. Accordingly Congress in 1850 had been driven to adopt a new principle—a sound one as Breckinridge saw it—and applied it to the newly organized territories of New Mexico and Utah. This principle was noninterference by Congress with slavery in the new territories, "leaving them free to form their own institutions, and enter the Union with or without slavery, as their constitutions should prescribe."

The Kentuckian then took notice of the widely circulated charge that the bill "proposes to legislate slavery into Nebraska and Kansas. Sir," he proclaimed, "if the bill contained such a feature, it could not receive my vote. The right to establish involves the correlative right to prohibit, and denying both, I would vote for neither." The effect of repealing the Missouri Compromise prohibition, he urged, "is neither to establish nor to exclude [slavery], but to leave the future condition of the Territories dependent wholly on the action of the inhabitants, subject only to such limitations as the Federal Constitution may impose."

Breckinridge admitted that there were two contending views among supporters of nonintervention by Congress and of popular sovereignty. One held that territorial legislatures "cannot rightfully exclude slavery" but that the people of a territory "may establish or prohibit it when they come to exercise the power of a sovereign State." This view was widely accepted in the South. The other, usually stigmatized as "squatter sovereignty" by its opponents, "claimed that the local Legislature may establish or exclude it any time after government is organized." The holders of both positions, he continued, "base their respective arguments on opposite constructions" of the Constitution. Accordingly the bill took the issue out of the hands of Congress and left it, as Breckinridge thought it should, to the federal judiciary, the normal agency for the determining of property rights under the Constitution.

Breckinridge had opened his speech on the Kansas-Nebraska Bill with an unnecessary attack upon Francis B. Cutting, a one-term member from New York City and one of the "Hard" faction of the New York Democracy.[8] A few days earlier Cutting had moved successfully that the bill, which had recently passed the Senate, be referred to the Committee of the Whole. Cutting, Breckinridge charged, professed to be a friend of the measure, but by his motion he had effectively buried it. He likened the New Yorker to a man who, with an arm around the shoulder of an unsuspecting friend, plunges a dagger into his heart. Cutting naturally resented Breckinridge's remarks and on March 27 he rose to defend himself. The immediate result was a bitter running interchange in which the two members offered strikingly different interpretations of the bill's chances in the light of the procedural rules of the House. More seriously, the interchange brought them close to a duel which might well have ended the careers of both men.

In the course of his remarks, Cutting suggested that

Breckinridge was guilty of ingratitude in making an "assault" upon him, since "in the day of the gentleman's greatest need, the 'Hards' of New York were those who came to his aid." When Breckinridge demanded the point of this innuendo, Cutting uttered what was in 1854 the unutterable:

> I am informed that, during the canvass in Kentucky, it being intimated that funds would be needed in order to accomplish the success of the gentleman, we—my friends in New York, the hards—made up a subscription of some $1,500, and transmitted the fund to Kentucky, to be employed for the benefit of the gentleman. . . .

Breckinridge immediately denied that he had personally requested or received any money from New York. "I was engaged," he cried,

> in an arduous and heated canvass, and was but little at home. My friends managed the canvass for me while I was traversing the district by day and by night, addressing assemblies of the people. I do not undertake to say what the fact may be in regard to this contemptible charge—it is enough to say that it touches me personally nowhere—and that I asked nothing and received nothing. No, sir; I came here not by the aid of money, but in spite of it. . . . It was loudly proclaimed in the public streets of the city in which I live that I should be defeated if it cost $50,000 to do it, and I can tell the member from New York that at least $30,000 was spent for that purpose. . . .

After Breckinridge had devoted some time to a further denunciation of Cutting, the latter resumed his defense of his course and quite unreasonably used the word "skulks" in referring to one aspect of Breckinridge's argument. Breckinridge asked Cutting to withdraw the offending word, to which Cutting replied with hyperbole, "I withdraw nothing that I have uttered. What I have said has been in answer to the most violent and most personal attack that has been witnessed upon this floor."

To this Breckinridge replied by giving Cutting the lie, "If the gentleman says that I skulk, he says what is false, and he knows it." Cutting reciprocated in the stilted language of the dueling code: "I do not, sir, upon this floor, answer remarks such as the member from Kentucky has just made. It belongs to a different arena. . . ."

Not surprisingly, Cutting that evening sent Breckinridge a crisp note, which Breckinridge interpreted as a challenge to a duel. Though the new Kentucky Constitution prohibited a duelist from holding office in the commonwealth, Breckinridge dared not refuse a challenge, as he valued his reputation for courage. Both parties named seconds and the correspondence moved forward punctiliously, step by step, while friends worked feverishly to bring about a peaceable settlement. On March 29, Breckinridge's second, T. T. Hawkins, proposed that the affair be settled that afternoon on or near Silver Spring, the Maryland estate of Francis P. Blair; he named as the weapon an "ordinary western rifle, with one charge of powder and one ball," the duelists to be separated by sixty paces. At this point Cutting's second complained that his principal was "wholly unacquainted" with the weapon proposed. Asserting Cutting's "rights as the challenged party," he demanded ordinary dueling pistols at ten paces.

This exchange put a new light on the matter. Hawkins replied that Breckinridge considered himself the challenged party. His opposite number assured him that Cutting's first note had not been intended as a challenge but merely as a request for an explanation. Thereafter the matter quickly unraveled. Breckinridge in the fourteenth note of the series, wrote of the third note (which Hawkins had earlier refused to receive) "that the disavowal it contains of an intention on your part to be personal in the language which led to my remark, is satisfactory, and I willingly withdraw the expressions which I used in reply." In a final note on March 31, Cutting joined Breckinridge in "reciprocating the sentiments of regret that any misunderstanding should have taken place, and of satisfaction at its happy ending." Thus narrowly was a duel averted and the honor of both parties preserved. That day in Kentucky Breckinridge's wife gave birth to their sixth child, a daughter presently named Mary Desha.

On April Fools' Day Breckinridge started for Kentucky to see his wife and the new arrival. During his visit the *Kentucky Statesman* published in full all fifteen of the notes written by Breckinridge, Cutting, and their seconds. Breckinridge's standing at home was somehow enhanced by what looks to the present-day reader like a provocative and useless attack on a fellow Democrat and by the defiant position which he took in the debate and correspondence which followed. After a three-week stay in Kentucky, Breckinridge returned to Washington. When the Kansas-Nebraska Bill finally passed the House of Representatives on May 22, by a vote 113 to 100, both Breckinridge and Cutting voted with the majority.

What Breckinridge's wife thought about his approach to a duel may readily be surmised. Some of his friendly constituents thought that he had not properly considered her situation and that of his children. One suggested that it had been a mistake to put himself on a level with a man who would make the charge Cutting had. William Birney, the special playmate of Breckinridge's school days, wrote affectionately from Philadelphia and urged that he avoid future approaches to a duel. Still Birney thought his old friend's "present position . . . an enviable one—on the whole rather improved by the late difficulty, since it has attracted to you the eyes of the nation."

Breckinridge was by now widely considered one of the rising young men of his party. But in February, 1854, the Whig majority in Kentucky's General Assembly passed over Governor Powell's veto a redistricting bill which removed "Sweet Owen" from the Eighth Congressional

District and replaced it with Harrison and Nicholas counties. Defending the measure, D. Howard Smith, a young Georgetown attorney who was a personal friend of Breckinridge and a Whig leader in the legislature, claimed that it was necessary to add a county to the district in order to bring it up to the average population of other districts. Though both Harrison and Nicholas usually voted Democratic, Breckinridge and his political supporters thought the motivation much more simple; the change was designed, they believed, to make his reelection impossible.

By January, 1855, another development threatened Breckinridge's prospects in the Ashland district. The American party, alias the Know-Nothing lodges, had made its appearance in Kentucky the previous year. One need not interpret the new phenomenon as primarily a hostile reaction against all the old parties and politicians, as one recent writer does, to understand the consternation which it caused among the old parties, but particularly among Democratic leaders at every level.[9] In Breckinridge's district, gerrymandered, as he saw it, to reduce the Democratic majority, most of the members of the secret order who had earlier been active in politics were Whigs. But local leaders reported that some Democrats had also joined. The overall effect was to make his reelection very doubtful indeed. On the other hand, his political mentors back home felt that he was the only Democrat who had a chance in the district.

At this juncture President Pierce, without consulting him until he was about to submit his name to the Senate, nominated Breckinridge as minister to Spain. At Madrid he would replace Pierre Soulé of Louisiana. Soulé's clumsy efforts to bring about the annexation of Cuba and his indefensible meddling in Spanish politics had long since ended his usefulness as an envoy to the Spanish government. Frustrated by failure and by a well-earned rebuke from Secretary of State Marcy, he had resigned in late December.

At once congratulations to Breckinridge poured in. Here was an honorable opportunity to avoid a possibly— probably—unsuccessful race for reelection. The minister-designate had all the tact and discretion which Soulé lacked. Many of his friends supposed that he could save money on the princely salary of $9,000 a year, plus an equal amount in the first year for an "outfit." His lack of fluency in either Spanish or French was not considered a handicap; neither was the fact that he had never made even a casual visit to Europe. The Senate hastened to confirm the nomination. But Breckinridge was in no hurry; on February 8, 1855, after some three weeks' consideration and consultation with his wife and friends, he declined the office. His reasons, he wrote Pierce, were "of a private and domestic nature."

Now the more sanguine of his surprised Kentucky supporters insisted that he had no choice but to declare himself a candidate for reelection to Congress. But again he was in no hurry to embark upon an exhausting and expensive canvass or to announce his decision. Congress adjourned on March 3 and soon Breckinridge was at home. He was warmly applauded, March 15, when he spoke at the state Democratic convention. That assembly nominated his good friend Magoffin for lieutenant governor and Beverly L. Clarke of Simpson County, a henchman of Speaker Linn Boyd, for governor. Two days later Breckinridge penned a letter to the editor of the *Kentucky Statesman* in which he formally declined to make another race for Congress. Again his announced reasons were "purely private and domestic"—in fact, his wife's uncertain health and his need to recoup his finances by returning to full-time law practice. A Philadelphia friend expressed his delight "That Mrs. B[.'s] good sense and judgment has prevailed over your *vagabondish political tendencies* and that you have determined to take care of her and the little children." Breckinridge was not much given to accepting his mother's counsel, but she too, more than a year earlier, had advised him in the strongest possible terms to abandon politics and get to work at his profession. "Look at Mr. Crittenden," she wrote, "he had to marry to keep from starving."[10]

In fulfillment of his purpose to make money, Breckinridge announced on April 3 that he had entered into a new partnership for the practice of law in Fayette and surrounding counties. His new associate was James Birnie Beck, a canny, hardworking young Scot who had nine years of practice to his credit. The firm of Kinkead and Breckinridge, to the great regret of the senior partner, had been dissolved eighteen months earlier when it appeared that Breckinridge's public responsibilities would make it impossible for him to give due attention to his practice.

In a further effort to increase his resources, Breckinridge had already begun to turn his attention to the West. If he had had no previous interest in land speculation, he could hardly have remained indifferent to its possibilities after he became well acquainted with Senator Douglas. The Little Giant bore him no grudge for his mistaken attempt in 1852 to hold him responsible for George N. Sanders's attack on Butler. In the summer of that year he called Breckinridge's attention to the possibilities of gain through investment in land around Chicago. Breckinridge, exploring the matter with Kinkead, proposed a joint investment under Douglas's guidance, but nothing came of this proposal. When Beck, who also had a keen interest in land speculation, visited Chicago in May, 1854, he reported to Breckinridge that prices thereabouts were altogether too high for profitable investment. Minnesota, northern Iowa, and northern Wisconsin, he wrote, offered the best prospects for farsighted investors.

During the congressional session beginning in December, 1853, the fascinating Breckinridge became a close friend of an equally fascinating contemporary, redheaded Henry M. Rice, new delegate from Minnesota Territory. Rice was an old Indian trader and land speculator, a man of boundless energy and ambition, who had amassed a considerable fortune and won the latest trick in the politics of the territory. He had also conceived a strong dislike for the new territorial governor, Willis A. Gorman, who in turn thought the worst of Rice. The Minnesota delegate soon proposed to guide Breckinridge along the way to wealth through investment in western lands.

In 1853 the prospect of a ship canal at Sault Sainte Marie which would enable large boats to move freely from Lake Huron into Lake Superior attracted the attention of Rice, Douglas, and other avid speculators to the western end of Lake Superior. Two rival groups, led by Douglas and Rice respectively, joined forces to preempt 6,000 acres on the Wisconsin side of the Saint Louis River, a site which had the advantage of a magnificent natural harbor on the lake.

Early in 1854, with the backing of banker William Corcoran, they organized the Superior Land Company. The original roll of shareholders read like a roster of Democratic luminaries and their connections. Besides Corcoran himself, it included Rice, Douglas, Bright, Robert J. Walker of Mississippi, Sen. Robert M. T. Hunter of Virginia, a brother-in-law of Douglas, a nephew of Sen. Lewis Cass, William A. Richardson (Douglas's lieutenant in the House of Representatives), Breckinridge, his crony John W. Forney of Pennsylvania (clerk of the House of Representatives and editor of the Washington *Union*), and four Minnesotans with money to invest but no established place in national politics.

Many of the shares were soon divided and subdivided. In September, 1854, Magoffin and Dr. Paul Rankins of Georgetown, whose wife was a sister of Mary Cyrene Breckinridge, set forth on an investigating trip which took them by rail via Indianapolis and Chicago to Galena, Illinois. From there they traveled up the Mississippi by steamboat to Saint Paul. Then they took the painful overland route to the town site on Lake Superior. They found that Superior City was gaining inhabitants rapidly. Before their return they purchased land near Saint Paul jointly for themselves, Breckinridge, and Isaac Shelby of Fayette County. At Superior each arranged to take a third of Breckinridge's share in the Superior Land Company.

Meanwhile in the long session of the Thirty-third Congress the Superior investors failed in a vigorous effort to procure a railroad land grant designed to give Superior a rail connection. The railroad was projected to run from Dubuque, Iowa, opposite the northwestern terminal of the Illinois Central Railroad, and through Saint Paul toward Lake Superior. The obvious boost which the rail connection would give his investment in Superior City led Breckinridge to favor the land grant. He had no part, however, in a bit of sharp practice by which the bill, once passed, was altered with Forney's consent before it was transmitted to the Senate. When Governor Gorman and others exposed the fraud, a congressional investigation was demanded. With adjournment near at hand Breckinridge, for the investigating committee, presented a bland majority report which condemned the practice of altering a bill after its passage. He further identified Forney and a member from Michigan as the responsible parties, but rather generously absolved "them of any criminal or improper purpose." On the last day of the session the altered bill was repealed.

Thus thwarted, the Superior speculators, working through Rice, Douglas, and Bright, joined forces in 1855 to persuade Pierce to remove Gorman and appoint Breckinridge in his place. The president, who had already demonstrated a desire to do something for the Kentuckian, professed to be willing. But two successive special investigators whom he sent to Minnesota could uncover nothing against Gorman which would warrant his removal. Long after Congress adjourned Rice lingered in Washington and New York in a fruitless effort to accomplish his purpose. Through the spring months he and Guthrie kept Breckinridge in close touch with developments. But in the end Gorman served out his term, and Breckinridge was not distracted from the task of strengthening his financial base.

With this end in view he took his first personal look at his investments in the Northwest. Late in May, 1855, relieved of his congressional duties and of the need to campaign for reelection, he and his wife set out for that region. On the urgent invitation of the Rices, Mrs. Breckinridge remained in Saint Paul with Mrs. Rice, while the two men traveled overland to Superior to check on their interests there. Breckinridge returned by way of the lakes to Detroit and thence by rail to Chicago and Galena, where he met his wife and escorted her home after an absence of nearly eight weeks. During that time he had expanded his investments. First at Rice's urging he bought land at Prairie du Chien, Wisconsin, on the Mississippi River. There land values were looking up with the approach of a railroad from Milwaukee. He also increased his holdings near Saint Paul and for $10,000 he bought an additional half share in Superior. Sharing the risk as well as the cost, he made each of his new purchases on a cooperative basis. Thus David R. Burbank, a Henderson friend of Governor Powell, was co-owner of his new Saint Paul acquisitions. Breckinridge shared his purchase at Prairie du Chien and his new half share in the Superior speculation with his eager new law partner. Earlier that year, in cooperation with Magoffin, Rankins, and a Minnesota friend, Breckinridge had purchased land on Basswood Island, one of the Apostles group in Lake Superior, close to the most northerly peninsula of mainland Wisconsin.

During his last three months as a congressman and after his return to Lexington in March, 1855, Breckinridge received numerous reports on the political situation. Some of his political friends urged the importance of his taking a strong stand against the Know-Nothing order, while others, including his stoutly nativist and anti-Catholic Uncle Robert, besought him to do nothing of the kind. In the end he rejected his uncle's counsel and accepted that of his fellow Democrats. At Cynthiana on April 21 he took a firm and statesmanlike position against the Know-Nothings. He denounced as un-American their program of denying voting privileges to immigrants and the right to hold public office to both naturalized citizens and Roman Catholics. He decried the selection of nominees for office and the determination of public policy by a secret, oath-bound society, led in large part, he said, by broken-down political hacks. He asserted that Know-Nothingism in the North had already resulted in election to Congress of no less than a hundred extreme abolitionists, many of them in place of northern Democrats who had stood loyally by the South in the crises of 1850 and 1854.

During his excursion to the Northwest, Breckinridge's political friends in Kentucky had all but demanded his early return to take an active part in the gubernatorial and congressional canvass leading to the election on August 6. When he did return late in July, both he and his wife were sick. He did manage, nevertheless, to keep seven speaking engagements during the final week of the campaign, two in Fayette County, and one each in Franklin, Scott, Harrison, Nicholas, and Jessamine counties. After voting he went to bed to recover from his illness, fatigue, and chagrin at the victory of the despised Know-Nothings. For governor they had elected Charles S. Morehead of Frankfort, Breckinridge's Whig predecessor as representative of the Eighth District. They had carried all the other state offices and had picked six "American" representatives to sit in the Thirty-fourth Congress. Most of the Know-Nothing candidates in Kentucky had been Whigs, though Breckinridge's successor in Congress, "American" A. K. Marshall, was an ex-Democrat. Marshall, an impecunious Nicholasville physician, had begged Breckinridge as recently as January, 1854, to help him find an office—almost any office—which would enable him to support his family.

As Breckinridge got back on his feet physically, he registered in letters to friends in Washington his deep embarrassment at the outcome of the election. Had he taken his usual aggressive part throughout the campaign, it might have turned out otherwise. His fervent assurances that the state would be redeemed in 1856 may have reflected a sense of guilt at his absence during most of the contest.

His absence had not lessened demands for his professional services. "I am in full practice—better than I ever had," he wrote Forney on August 12. His practice emphasized courtroom appearances, not only in Fayette County and before the Court of Appeals at Frankfort, but also in the circuit courts of most of the counties within a radius of thirty miles from Lexington. With a partner like Beck, who excelled in the preparation of cases for trial, he could devote himself, much of the time, to oral argument.

If Breckinridge ever intended to give all his working time to his profession and his investments, he early found it impossible to disengage himself from politics. Soon he was engaged in planning a great Democratic mass convention to be held at Lexington, October 5, to lay the foundations for victory in 1856. He persuaded Douglas, Sen. George E. Pugh of Cincinnati, and Lieutenant Governor Willard of Indiana to come for the occasion. When the day arrived, he called to order a crowd of four to five thousand people, assembled on the grounds of Transylvania University. He served on the resolutions committee, which reported an address to the voters and a set of resolutions. Those of the resolutions which dealt with national issues had been drafted by Douglas.[11] They firmly endorsed the Compromise of 1850 and the Kansas-Nebraska Bill, denounced the Know-Nothing movement, and heartily welcomed those former Whigs who, repudiating it, were prepared to cooperate with the Democrats.

3

THE YOUNGEST
VICE PRESIDENT

The THIRTEEN SCANT years between the Mexican War and the Civil War in which Breckinridge came to maturity and won a surprising succession of political victories were a time of recurrent crises. So they seemed to contemporaries and so they appear to the student who analyzes the steps which in retrospect seem to lead inexorably to the conflict which rent the country asunder.

Though Breckinridge had urged that the Kansas-Nebraska Bill would take the slavery issue out of national politics and assuage the strife between the sections, it had a contrary effect. By 1856 antislavery forces, stirred to action by passage of the bill, had coalesced as the Republican party. The new party was not committed, whatever Breckinridge and his political friends might charge, to the abolition of slavery in the states. Nor would it settle for the restoration of the Missouri Compromise line in the territories. Rather it stood for the principle that Congress had the power and duty to prohibit slavery in all the territories. Thus slavery might be contained within the fifteen slaveholding states.

To Breckinridge, and even more to defenders of slavery in the lower South, such a program threatened the southern way of life. To Breckinridge, Douglas, and many another observer, the existence of a party advocating such a program gravely menaced the Union itself. Numerous leaders from the deep South made as clear in 1856 as in 1860 their conviction that election of a Republican president on a platform calling for the containment of the peculiar institution would amply justify the secession of the slave states. Though Breckinridge did not personally take this ground, he had some basis for thinking that a victory of his own party—still strong in all sections—was the best hope for the preservation of the Union he loved.

During the late autumn of 1855, however, to the extent that he spared time from his law practice and his personal concerns, he was immediately preoccupied with preparations for the Democratic state convention. Called for the traditional date, January 8, it was to select delegates to the national convention at Cincinnati in June. Breckinridge and his closest political friends were determined to keep the convention from binding delegates to any presidential candidate and particularly to avoid an endorsement of "the Mogul of the 1st," former Speaker Linn Boyd. Looking forward to the state conclave, Breckinridge corresponded with numerous political friends and exhorted the conventions of Fayette and Jessamine counties. Of his speech at the latter convention, December 17, an admiring reporter wrote, "The speech was a great and masterly effort of a master mind in defence of the principles of the Kansas and Nebraska Bill, and the nationality of the Democratic party."

When the state convention met, the Powell-Breckinridge forces were powerful but not in command. They did succeed in preventing any expressed preference for Boyd as candidate for president. Breckinridge, Colonel Preston, and the recent candidates for governor and lieutenant governor, Clarke and Magoffin, were named delegates at large to the national convention. Breckinridge and Elijah Hise of Russellville, who was just completing a term as chief justice of the Court of Appeals, were chosen as electors at large. This assignment would require them to canvass the state for the nominees of the Cincinnati convention. The platform adopted was identical in its principal provisions with that drafted by Douglas for the Lexington mass meeting the previous October, and with platforms adopted in several other states at his instance.

During the interval between the conventions Breckinridge received a melange of information and misinformation about the strengths of the several candidates. He was courted by friends of the three principal prospects, President Pierce, Senator Douglas, and James Buchanan, who had resigned his mission to the United Kingdom and reached New York in April. Douglas, convalescing in Cleveland after throat surgery, assumed that the Kentuckian was in his camp. Accordingly he authorized one of his Ohio lieutenants to solicit Breckinridge's advice. Secretary of the Treasury Guthrie wrote from Washington supporting the president's claim to a second nomination. From Baton Rouge the husband of one of Mary Cyrene Breckinridge's first cousins asked whether John would be willing to run for vice president, presumably on a ticket with Buchanan. That gentleman's claims were pushed more directly by Breckinridge's closest Pennsylvania friends, John W. Forney and George H. Martin of Philadelphia.

When the balloting began at Cincinnati, the twenty-four members of the Kentucky delegation divided their twelve votes among the three principal contenders. After the seventh ballot no Kentucky votes were cast for Pierce, whose support was transferred to Douglas. On the fourteenth ballot at the end of the first day of voting, the Kentuckians stood 4½ for Buchanan and 7½ for Douglas, while the convention as a whole recorded 152½ votes for Buchanan, 75 for Pierce, and 63 for Douglas.

Overnight a vigorous effort was made to concentrate the Pierce-Douglas strength on Douglas, but it failed. On the sixteenth ballot Kentucky, voting unanimously for the first time, gave her 12 votes to Douglas, who then reached his maximum strength with 122. At that juncture Preston, an earnest Douglas supporter, reluctantly proposed the withdrawal of the senator's name and gained the floor for William A. Richardson, Douglas's recognized spokesman. Thereupon Richardson, over the indignant protests of many Douglas men, read a message from the Little Giant, authorizing the withdrawal of his name in the interest of party unity, majority rule, and a victory for the principles incorporated in the platform. Thus on the seventeenth ballot, Buchanan was chosen unanimously.

Breckinridge voted for Pierce early in the balloting and then switched to Douglas. Magoffin, who roomed with Breckinridge at the convention, soon traveled to Washington to look out for the interests of the Superior speculators. He also had an opportunity to correct a report which had reached Pierce's friends that Breckinridge had not voted for him on any ballot. Though a postconvention attempt had been made "to poison Douglas' mind" against Breckinridge, a man whom he trusted had reassured him of the Kentuckian's "fidelity." Magoffin personally told Douglas of Breckinridge's negative response when some of the Pennsylvania delegates in Magoffin's hearing had proposed a coalition between the supporters of Buchanan and the friends of Breckinridge.[1]

Buchanan was nominated on the morning of June 6. That afternoon the convention proceeded to select a vice-presidential nominee. For the Kentucky delegation, ex-Governor Charles A. Wickliffe nominated Boyd. An Illinoisan proposed Gen. John A. Quitman of Mississippi, and a Louisiana delegate nominated Breckinridge. At once Breckinridge gained the floor, modestly thanked the Louisianians, but indicated his belief in promotion by seniority and declined to run in competition with his delegation's nominee, "a tried and able champion of the Democracy." Breckinridge added that he was already a candidate for elector. In that capacity he looked forward to an "active campaign—to traverse the valleys and climb the mountains of my native State, in behalf of the distinguished and noble candidate we have already selected for the Presidency, and in advocacy of the glorious States Rights Platform, which we have adopted with singular unanimity."

On the first ballot votes were cast for ten different men. Quitman led with fifty-nine votes. Eight delegations, impressed by Breckinridge's remarks and style, brushed aside his refusal and put him in second place with fifty-five votes. Boyd ran third with thirty-three, including Kentucky's twelve. On the second ballot Breckinridge was far in the lead when, with contagious enthusiasm, one state after another withdrew its favorite and transferred its votes to him. Finally he was declared the unanimous choice of the convention.

Sen. John Slidell of Louisiana, mastermind of the Buchanan candidacy, wrote Breckinridge ten days later and claimed that he had urged his state's delegation to propose Breckinridge in response to the "earnest appeal of Richardson." He went on to say, "I considered your selection for the Vice Presidency a graceful and merited compliment to the friends of Douglas." There is no reason to question the veracity of Slidell's statement. In any event the nomination made sense for the reason he stated and in other ways as well. A vigorous, "graceful" young orator of thirty-five would give dash and even color to a ticket headed by a stuffy elder statesman of sixty-five. Tradition and partisan common sense required a southerner to balance the candidacy of the Pennsylvania squire. Many delegates who had not previously known Breckinridge liked what they saw and heard when he modestly tried to remove his name from consideration. Though the author of the Kansas-Nebraska Bill had been passed by, the convention, in naming Breckinridge, had chosen a man closely identified with Douglas and one who had worked hard to pass the bill. And Kentucky was a doubtful state whose votes might prove essential to victory.

With the vice-presidential nominee on the convention floor, the delegates at once called him out. His remarks in response were brief, but the weary crowd enjoyed a chance to hear the magnetic Kentuckian return thanks in gracious terms and announce again in ringing tones his earnest support of Buchanan and the party's platform. They applauded everything he said, including his reaffirmation of his position as a "states' rights man."

Back in February the American party had split over the issue of slavery in the territories. When its nominating convention at Philadelphia rejected a resolution that no candidate be nominated who did not favor the prohibition of slavery in the territories north of the old Missouri Compromise line of 36°30′, most of the antislavery delegates walked out. Ultimately they threw their support to the Republican nominee. The remnant, consisting largely of southerners, nominated ex-President Fillmore for president. Finally and most ominously, as the Democrats saw it, the convention of the new Republican party met in Philadelphia a week after the adjournment of the Cincinnati meeting. It called for the federal prohibition of slavery and polygamy in all the territories, and named John C. Frémont, the explorer, as its standard-bearer. Thus began the campaign—between Buchanan and Fillmore in the fifteen slave states, and primarily between Frémont and Buchanan in the other sixteen states.

Had Breckinridge accepted all the invitations urging him to speak at this rally or merely to show himself at that barbecue, he would have been on the road throughout the five months between the adjournment of the Democratic convention and the November election. As a matter of fact he spent most of that period at home in Kentucky. At Cincinnati, the night of his nomination, serenaded by the brass band of the Pennsylvania delegation, he had spoken briefly to the crowd which accompanied the musicians. Ten days later a Democratic "ratification meeting" at Lexington sent a committee to bring him from his home to the rally. Again he acknowledged the plaudits of the crowd and spoke briefly but enthusiastically of Buchanan's qualifications and the party platform. There could be no serious objection to such appearances as these, but Breckinridge at first felt some delicacy about full-length speechmaking for the "Buck and Breck" ticket. Friends and well-wishers soon convinced him, however, that there was precedent for speaking on behalf of the party ticket by a vice-presidential nominee. Responding to a series of pressing invitations, he made an exhausting expedition during the first ten days of September. The excursion took him as a featured speaker to Hamilton, Ohio, and to huge Democratic rallies at the Tippecanoe Battlefield in Indiana, at Kalamazoo, Michigan, and finally at Pittsburgh. Enroute he could not avoid speaking briefly to enthusiastic crowds of partisans at Covington, Kentucky, Cincinnati, and Indianapolis. Following his Pittsburgh appearance he made a quick trip to Wheatland to confer with Buchanan.

In the Tippecanoe address Breckinridge spoke earnestly of the threat to the Union which he saw in the Republican party and its program. "He must be blind indeed, and given over to fatal delusion, who does not see that the Union of the States is in imminent peril," he cried. "Crossing the narrow Ohio to a sister State, we find a large portion . . . of the people maddened with excitement and hurling every epithet of hate and ignominy against their brethren of the South. The sectional hostility thus aroused is fed," he added, "by misrepresentations of the opinions and feelings of the Southern people."

The Kentuckian charged that the Republican party's objects "reach far beyond any solution of the questions relating to Nebraska and Kansas." Its "ulterior purpose," he said, "is to bring the Federal Government into active aggression upon slavery in the States, and to combine public opinion and political action in such a form as to abolish the institution wherever it exists. This purpose," he warned, "is openly avowed by the bolder leaders of the party." "Fellow citizens," he continued,

I solemnly appeal to every man who loves his country—who believes that the Union of the States has been the source of their unexampled prosperity and happiness, and that dissolution would be the end of both—to pause and consider, in the spirit of a patriot the present condition of public affairs.

The young orator recalled Washington's farewell advice to cherish the Union and oppose all attempts "to alienate any portion of our country from the rest." He identified the Republican party as an example of a sectional party against which the father of the country had warned. Then he appealed to the spirit of Henry Clay— his love for the whole country and his fear "that the agitation of the question [of slavery] in the free states will first destroy all harmony, and finally lead to disunion, perpetual war, the extinction of the African race, and ultimate military despotism."

Breckinridge defended the Kansas-Nebraska Bill in language much like that which he had now been using for two years. With a casual reference he brushed aside "the disturbances engendered by designing men through folly or ambition" which had accompanied the attempt to apply the doctrine of popular sovereignty in Kansas. He praised the measure for including the true American principle, asserted from colonial days, that the "inhabitants" of a territory were "competent to manage their own affairs."[2] Though he did not in so many words endorse the "squatter sovereignty" interpretation of the bill, commonly held by those northern Democrats who supported the measure, the language he used was close enough to bring him sharp criticism from American party spokesmen and newspapers in the South.

Breckinridge's admirers discounted the criticism and valued his speeches as a significant contribution to the ultimate victory of the ticket. More important, however, was his part in strengthening the organization of his party in Kentucky. Another major contribution was his deployment in Pennsylvania and other northern states of Kentucky spellbinders, especially such ex-Whigs as Preston and James B. Clay, son of the Whig idol. A voluminous correspondence kept him in touch with developments across the nation, particularly in the states where he had personally campaigned. His exchanges with Buchanan, initially rather stilted on both sides, gradually took on something approaching easy good fellowship in the common cause, particularly after their brief consultation in September. Throughout the campaign Breckinridge assured Buchanan that he might depend upon Kentucky's vote, certainly if the party should carry Pennsylvania, as it did, in the state election of October 14.

To make good his pledge, he worked assiduously with a rather ineffectual state central committee and with W. W. Stapp, a vigorous newspaperman whom prominent Louisville Democrats tardily sent to Frankfort about the first of October to stiffen the committee and serve as its executive officer. Breckinridge also arranged for the circulation of appropriate government documents among the voters. He helped assign speakers—veteran Democrats and a small platoon of ex-Whigs—and received reports and counsel from them and from others of the faithful scattered throughout the state. He corresponded with party editors and stimulated the raising of funds for a lean campaign chest.

But November 4 brought triumph for "Buck and Breck," who won 174 electoral votes against 114 for Frémont and 8 for Fillmore. The Democrats carried all the slaveholding states except Maryland, which provided Fillmore's only electoral votes. In addition they won by tiny majorities in Pennsylvania and Indiana and by comfortable pluralities in New Jersey, Illinois, and California.

Particularly sweet for Breckinridge was the victory in Kentucky, which for the first time since 1828 voted for the Democratic nominees. The hard-fought campaign had brought them 74,642 votes (approximately 52.4 percent of the total), Fillmore 67,416, and Frémont 314. These figures represented a much larger voter turnout than in 1852. The Democratic vote was nearly 21,000 higher than Pierce's; though the American party lost many voters who had supported General Scott in 1852, it turned out for Fillmore in 1856 about 10,000 more votes than the Whigs had polled for the general.

All but six of the forty-three counties which had voted Democratic in 1852 gave their votes to Buchanan and Breckinridge four years later, most of them with a substantial increase in Democratic strength. The increases were spectacular in some, notably the mountain counties of Letcher, Floyd, Johnson, Breathitt, and Morgan, and centrally located Washington. In Washington a large Roman Catholic element reacted unfavorably to Fillmore's running as a Know-Nothing. In Washington's neighbors, Marion and Nelson counties, the Catholic response to Know-Nothingism played a major part in transforming Whig majorities of 50.6 percent and 66.3 percent respectively in 1852 into Democratic majorities of 73.4 percent and 56.8 percent in 1856. Comparable party shifts, without any particular religious connotation, took place in six more mountain counties—Pike, Perry, Estill, Lawrence, Wayne, and Pulaski—and in eight counties of western and southern Kentucky.[3]

Because Breckinridge throughout his public career stood guard for the rights of slaveholders, it is natural to suppose that his greatest strength would lie in the counties where slaveholders constituted a large part of the electorate. But no positive correlation between slaveholding and allegiance to Breckinridge or his party can be found. In 1856, as well as in 1852 and 1860, Democrats and their opponents both carried counties in which a large proportion of the potential voters were slaveholders; both also carried counties in which the number of slaveholders was inconsequential. Of the eight mountain counties which gave the Democratic ticket from 72 percent to 98 percent of their vote in 1856, none had a significant number of slaves or slaveholders. In Johnson,

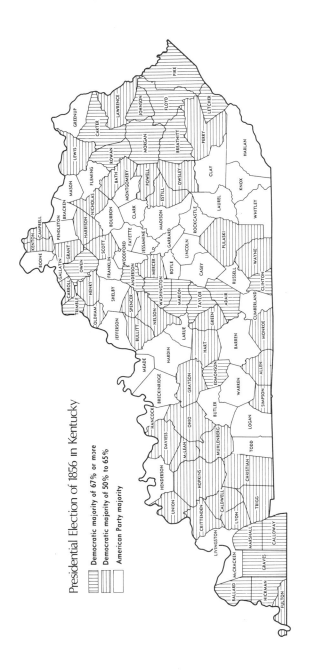

Presidential Election of 1856 in Kentucky

▥ Democratic majority of 67% or more

▤ Democratic majority of 50% to 65%

☐ American Party majority

the prime Democratic county in 1852, 1856, and 1860, only 1.09 percent of the potential voters of 1860 held slaves. But slaveholders were scarcely more numerous in the rugged counties of southeastern Kentucky, which were traditionally Whig and which in 1856 produced respectable majorities for Fillmore. Of the twenty-three principal slaveholding counties, Fillmore carried fourteen, "Buck and Breck" nine.

The four months between the election and the inauguration were busy for Breckinridge, whose prospective elevation had not lessened the demand for his professional services, particularly as a courtroom advocate. He received numerous letters of congratulation, many accompanied by the heartening prediction that in another four or eight years he would be advanced to the highest office in the land. Many requests for aid in procuring public employment, from cabinet positions to the humblest clerkships, reached his desk. In most cases he replied that he had resolved to make no requests and offer no advice regarding patronage until his counsel was asked. His own perquisites involved only two appointments, a private secretary and a page.

If the president-elect sought Breckinridge's advice at any time before the inauguration, the evidence has disappeared. On their way to Washington the vice president-elect and his wife spent a little over a week in Philadelphia. This stop afforded their friend and social mentor, George H. Martin, the opportunity to supervise the addition of some items to Breckinridge's wardrobe. At Philadelphia Breckinridge received an invitation from Buchanan, who proposed that the Breckinridges spend Sunday, March 1, with him at Wheatland and accompany him to Washington the next day. The major declined politely on the ground that it would be an intrusion to be his chief's guest the last day before his departure from home. But he accepted an alternate suggestion that they meet in Baltimore on the afternoon of March 2.

On inauguration day the customary routine was followed. Breckinridge became the youngest vice president in the history of the republic as he took his oath of office in the Senate Chamber at 12:30. He then moved to the outdoor platform where Buchanan took the oath and delivered his inaugural address. According to the admiring editor of the *Kentucky Statesman,* the vice president was greeted with "thunders of applause" when he took his place on the stand.

Three days after the inauguration Buchanan asked the vice president's advice about proposing James B. Clay as minister to Prussia. Should he send his name to the Senate for confirmation, as Pierce had Breckinridge's two years earlier, or should he first write Clay, offering him the post? Breckinridge advised the latter course, which Buchanan adopted, only to receive a courteous refusal a few days later.

Soon thereafter a misunderstanding arose between the two highest officers of the republic. The difficulty reflected Buchanan's social clumsiness or his frigidity of manner, or both, as well as the high-strung pride of the Kentuckian. Breckinridge had asked the president for a private interview and received in reply a suggestion that he call at the White House some evening and ask to see Miss Lane, Buchanan's niece and hostess. Taking the reply or the manner in which it was given as a brush-off, Breckinridge did not call on Miss Lane. Soon after the usual special session of the Senate adjourned, he returned to Kentucky without again seeing the president.

Breckinridge's resentment was soon reported to Buchanan, and no less than three persons who enjoyed the president's confidence wrote to explain that it was all a mistake. The intermediaries were Senator Bright, Secretary of War John B. Floyd, a distant kinsman of Breckinridge, and federal District Attorney J. C. Van Dyke of Philadelphia. They explained that a caller's request to see Miss Lane was in effect a password, in response to which he would at once be ushered into the presence of her uncle—a device to insure the private interview which

Breckinridge had sought. They also reported that the president deeply regretted the misunderstanding.

That spring and even during the preceding year the speculative bubble grew larger day by day. Unprecedentedly high prices were offered for property like Breckinridge's holdings at Superior, Saint Paul, Basswood Island, and Prairie du Chien. Under this stimulus the vice president sought further opportunities for advancing his fortune. In November and December, 1856, his hard-driving and sanguine partner made an expedition in search of joint investments within reach of the line of the Illinois Central Railroad in southern Illinois. Riding horseback and at times trudging on foot through rain and mud to make a personal examination of land under consideration, Beck periodically reported in writing. He exhorted Breckinridge to raise, as he presently did, more money to meet the early payments on the land for which Beck had contracted. He complained only that they could not raise more money to invest.

By the spring of 1857, the partners' joint funds for investment replenished, Beck was at it again. Hardly waiting for the vice president's return to Lexington, he hurried west, sought suitable purchases in the interior of Iowa along projected railroad routes, and bought at Prairie du Chien nineteen additional lots at a cost of $8,300. As soon as the Mississippi opened for the season, he pushed on to Saint Paul in search of further opportunities.

When Beck reached the Minnesota capital late in April, he found a letter in which Breckinridge directed that no new investments be made for him. This direction reflected no foresight that the speculative bubble would soon burst. Rather it resulted from the fact that Douglas, Rice, and Breckinridge had jointly purchased two blocks on I and New Jersey streets in Washington and that they were planning to build large, plain but expensive houses side by side on one of them. The vice president realized that he might find it difficult to make his share of the payments on the new Washington holdings while paying for building and furnishing his new home. Accordingly he thought it best to make no new commitments elsewhere and authorized Beck to sell for him a quarter share in the Superior project if a buyer could be found at the exorbitant figure of $25,000 cash.

Beck, however, failed to make a sale at Saint Paul or during a trip to Superior in July. By early August Breckinridge was prepared to sell a quarter share at from $15,000 to $18,000 on the down-to-earth thesis, expressed in a letter to Bright, that "when a man needs and *must have money,* whatever he has to sell is worth *just what it will bring.*" The financial pressure reflected by these words was serious enough; yet it would become worse, as a few significant business failures in late August were followed by more in September and by a full-blown panic in October.

Before the crash the sanguine Rice, who had all but pushed Breckinridge into the building program in Washington, had hoped to be able to carry for a time both Breckinridge's and his own share in the project. But by September 27 the Minnesotan was in desperate straits himself and could only advise his friend that it was better to borrow at any rate than to sell property at the going prices. By October 22 Rice had sustained further losses and was ready to sell his house, now approaching completion, in Washington.

Meanwhile Breckinridge's situation, so he wrote Rice on October 8, had eased somewhat. He had sold his Lexington home and the land surrounding it and had offered at auction several head of cattle, several horses, his "new light Rockaway" buggy, and some furniture and household goods. He also sold at least one female slave and her infant child. As the autumn wore on he realized $8,150 by selling two choice lots and a half share in ten more at Superior.

When the time came for the opening of the Thirty-fifth Congress, Breckinridge did not occupy his splendid new home on what was soon called Minnesota Row. Instead he escorted his wife and younger daughter from Lexington to Baton Rouge, Louisiana. There and at Lake Washington, Mississippi, Mary had arranged to spend the winter with kinfolk. Her plans had been completed so late that the Senate had been in session for two weeks when its presiding officer finally reached the capital. Then, like an ordinary member of Congress, he took lodgings at Mrs. French's house on Fifteenth Street near the White House.

In spite of his financial worries, Breckinridge had reason to rejoice in the results of the August elections in Kentucky. James B. Clay, now campaigning as a Democrat, had carried the Ashland district against a future Confederate brigadier, Roger W. Hanson. Another of Breckinridge's devoted personal and political friends, John W. Stevenson of Covington, won the race in the Tenth District, which since 1854 had embraced "Sweet Owen" and a string of counties along the Ohio River, above and below Covington. In fact the Democrats carried eight of the ten congressional districts in Kentucky. That and results of other August elections would assure the Democrats a majority in the Thirty-fifth Congress. Almost equally important to Breckinridge was the election of a legislature which would be safely Democratic on a joint ballot for a United States senator to replace Whig-American John B. Thompson for the term beginning March 4, 1859. The vice president had taken part in the detailed planning, even down to the selection of popular Democrats to run in this or that legislative district.

The senatorial election was held on January 5, 1858.[4] The real contest, between Breckinridge's political friends ex-Governor Powell and James Guthrie and his enemy Linn Boyd, took place in the Democratic caucus, which plumped for Powell. Accordingly the former governor received a unanimous party vote on the joint ballot. But Breckinridge's decision to support him, reached as early as September, had opened a rift in his relations with Guthrie. That rift would prove significant in 1860.

Like most of his predecessors in the office of vice president, Breckinridge played no significant part in the presidential administration. He stood ready to succeed to the presidency should Buchanan, like Harrison and Taylor, die in office. He presided modestly, gracefully, and impartially over the Senate. Occasionally he cast a tie-breaking vote. Rarely consulted, he had less part in shaping the policy of the administration than he had enjoyed in President Pierce's time. Indeed, the only recent scholarly biography of Buchanan barely mentions the vice president except as a nominee in 1860 for the succession. Yet, though his political insights and his gift for conciliation were wasted by a president who could have used both, he followed the administration line on the critical issue of the day—the political future of Kansas.

Hard pressed by southern extremists, Buchanan in December, 1857, recommended the admission of Kansas to the Union under the Lecompton Constitution. In short, he advocated the admission of Kansas as a slave state, following a referendum in which Kansas voters were given two options—"the constitution with slavery" and "the constitution without slavery."⁵ Free-soilers, by that time in a large majority, had boycotted the referendum, charging fraud in the election of the delegates who framed the constitution and denouncing the lack of an opportunity to reject the constitution as a whole. Hence the voters who went to the polls chose overwhelmingly "the constitution with slavery."

Douglas, appalled at what he deemed mockery of his popular sovereignty dogma, broke with the president. Supported by many northern Democrats, Senator Crittenden, several of the handful of American party members left in the House of Representatives, and some Republicans, he demanded resubmission of the Lecompton Constitution to a full and free referendum. But there were too few affirmative votes in the House of Representatives to admit Kansas under that charter without a fresh vote of the Kansans. Nor would the administration majority in the Senate consent to resubmission.

The upshot was a compromise in which Kansas voters were finally given an opportunity—disguised in other terms to save the president's face—to accept or reject the constitution as a whole. This ambiguous solution suited neither Douglas, nor the Republicans, nor the extreme advocates of southern rights, but it passed.[6] All eight Democratic members from Kentucky voted for it, while their two American party colleagues and Senator Crittenden were in the negative minority. Breckinridge, who had gone south to take his wife back to Kentucky, was absent at the time of the final vote, April 30, and through all the haggling of the previous month. But he and his political future were involved.

During the months of controversy Breckinridge was attacked by some of the opposition press for his failure to take a public stand on the Kansas question. Presently he suffered an attack for the stand he did take. After Congress adjourned in June, 1858, he returned to Kentucky and during July, in a series of speeches at Harrodsburg, Florence, Cynthiana, and Owenton, he declared that he had favored admission of Kansas under the Lecompton Constitution. On this and other issues he endorsed the president's policy. Like Buchanan, he defended on purely legalistic grounds the Lecompton Constitution and the failure to submit the document as a whole to a popular vote. He criticized as disloyal to southern interests those, like Crittenden, who had cooperated with the Republicans in defeating the plan to admit Kansas as a slave state. He made it clear that he still thought the Republican party a dangerous menace to the South and to the continuance of the Union. Looking toward the election of 1860, he predicted that the Democracy would be

Vice President John C. Breckinridge, about 1860
Courtesy of the Historical Society of Pennsylvania

the only party in the field against the "abolitionist" program of the Republicans. He called on all southern men, especially young men, to rally to the Democratic standard and thus to hearten northern opponents of the Republicans.

Breckinridge had refrained from attacking his old friend Douglas by name. He knew that Douglas was already embarked upon his long and critical campaign for reelection to the Senate, with Abraham Lincoln as his Republican opponent. Interest in the campaign reached its peak between August 21 and October 15, when Lincoln and Douglas engaged in their famous series of seven debates. Stressing the importance of defeating Lincoln, Robert J. Ward and other Breckinridge supporters in Kentucky urged him to speak out on behalf of Douglas. When word got out that the vice president was willing to do so, the chairman of the Democratic central committee of Illinois invited him to give a series of speeches at critical points in the state. Replying on October 4, Breckinridge wrote that he was not willing to "leave Kentucky for the purpose of mingling in the political discussions in other states." But he added that he had "often in conversation expressed the wish that Mr. Douglas may succeed over his Republican competitor." He warned, however, that this wish should not be taken as an endorsement of Douglas's "course at the last session of Congress . . . or of all the positions he has taken in the present canvass." He guardedly justified his preference for Douglas on the ground

that he seems to be the candidate of the Illinois Democracy, and the most formidable opponent in that state of the Republican party, and that on more than one occasion during his public life he has defended the Union of the states and the rights of the states with fidelity, courage, and great ability.

Breckinridge's letter was widely published. With similar endorsements by other southern and border-state

Democrats, especially ex-Whigs like James B. Clay, it may have contributed something to the election in November of a modest majority of Democratic legislators pledged to vote for Douglas's reelection. After the legislature had again conferred the senatorship on Douglas, the Little Giant, in spite of his feud with the president and his denunciation by many southern Democrats who blamed him for the loss of a slave state, stood forth as the strongest contender for the Democratic presidential nomination in 1860.

Breckinridge's reserved expression of preference for Douglas was less than satisfactory to the Little Giant and his supporters. On the other hand it did not improve his relations with Buchanan, whose henchmen had tardily put up a third candidate for the Illinois senatorship and who was adamant in his design to crush Douglas, whatever the cost.

On January 4, 1859, two days before Douglas's reelection, Breckinridge made a much admired brief address with no overt reference to the issues of the day. The occasion was the removal of the Senate from the old hall which it had occupied since 1819 to the newly completed chamber in the north wing of the Capitol. The vice president took the opportunity to indulge his taste for political history. He began by reviewing the numerous moves made by the Continental Congress, the Congress under the Articles of Confederation, and the Congress under the Constitution, and the controversies which preceded the permanent location of Congress at Washington in 1800. Then he moved to a brief history of the Senate itself, with special emphasis upon the careers of three of its greatest members—Calhoun, Webster, and Clay.

In the most impressive part of the address Breckinridge stressed the tremendous growth and progress which the United States had experienced during seventy years under the Constitution and the happy condition of their people compared with those of other lands. He praised the American political system and the men who had devised and maintained "this admirable Constitution, which has survived peace and war, prosperity and adversity; this double scheme of Government, State and Federal . . . , which protects the earnings of industry, and makes [possible] the largest personal freedom compatible with public order." He called down "the execrations of all mankind" upon any "American . . . who will deride his country's laws, pervert her Constitution, or alienate her people." He concluded:

And now, Senators, we leave this memorable Chamber, bearing with us, unimpaired, the Constitution we received from our forefathers. . . . These marble walls must molder into ruin; but the principles of constitutional liberty, guarded by wisdom and virtue, . . . do not decay. Let us devoutly trust that another Senate, in another age, shall bear to a new and larger Chamber, this Constitution, vigorous and inviolate, and that the last generation of posterity shall witness the deliberations of the Representatives of the American States still united, prosperous, and free.

Breckinridge's plea for perpetual union, harmony, and reverence for the Constitution and laws was more than timely. But it was little heeded during a year in which southern threats of secession became increasingly common and differences over the meaning of the Constitution became increasingly bitter.

4

THE CRISIS OF DISUNION

Many of the vice president's admirers had long predicted his advancement to the highest office in the land. But his political future was far from certain as with patriotic words he ushered in a year of bitter strife within his party and between the sections. Two obvious questions confronted him: What did he want and what could he get? The prizes were a senatorship from Kentucky for the term beginning March 4, 1861, and the presidency. Presidential electors would not be chosen until November, 1860; but Kentucky's senator would be elected by the legislature which was to convene in December, 1859, and to adjourn in March, 1860. Hence Breckinridge needed first to reach a decision on the senatorship. By January, 1859, some of his political intimates knew that he wished to be elected senator, whatever effect his candidacy might have on his presidential chances. He did not consider it prudent to be known as an aspirant for both positions simultaneously; indeed many Kentucky Democrats demanded, as a virtual prerequisite to the senatorship, that he commit himself to support for president their particular favorite—either Douglas or more commonly Guthrie, now president of the Louisville & Nashville Railroad.

Before Breckinridge or any Democrat could win the senatorship, however, it was necessary to elect a legislature which would again muster a Democratic majority. It was also highly desirable to elect a state ticket or at least a governor friendly to the would-be senator's aspirations. At the same time it was important not to alienate potential supporters by taking too strong a stand for the nomination of a particular gubernatorial candidate. It was important, if Breckinridge was to retain any faint hope for the presidency, that the state convention which nominated the state ticket adopt a platform which would not prove a liability to him. And it was desirable to retain a Democratic majority in the Kentucky delegation to the House of Representatives.

The first engagement of the campaign took place in Frankfort, where the state Democratic convention met on January 8, 1859. After the first ballot four men were still in the running for the gubernatorial nomination; but the real choice lay between Magoffin, still a warm Breckinridge man, and Boyd, now his bitter opponent. On the fifth ballot the delegates chose Magoffin, who had led from the start. The final vote was 363 to 305. Boyd was then nominated by acclamation for lieutenant governor. Many observers thought that he accepted second place because of the advantage which participation in a statewide canvass would give him in lining up votes for the senatorship.

The resolutions of the convention were "carefully scanned," a Kentucky advocate of Douglas for president assured him, to prevent a positive endorsement or denunciation of Buchanan's Lecompton policy. The convention rejected outright a plank calling for congressional adoption of a "slave code" for the territories, a measure which southern fire-eaters were beginning to demand. Buchanan was given "an empty compliment" but no outright commendation of his Kansas policy. The platform was one on which Douglas or Guthrie or Breckinridge could run without embarrassment.

Magoffin, Boyd, and the Democratic party carried the state election in August against an "Opposition" party which consisted chiefly of persistent Whigs, including most of the men who had borne the American party banner in 1855 and 1856. On the other hand the opposition took three of the eight congressional seats which the Democrats had won in 1857. Thus Kentucky would be represented in the new House of Representatives by five Democrats and five "Oppositionists." With a majority of ten in the state Senate and of eighteen in the state House of Representatives, the Democrats were clearly in a position to elect one of their own leaders to the United States Senate. Though Boyd was a very sick man and unable to go to Frankfort for the inauguration on August 30, he remained Breckinridge's chief opponent well into the fall. On November 28, however, he withdrew from the race; in less than three weeks he died at the age of fifty-nine.

Meanwhile the Democratic caucus met and on the first ballot it gave Breckinridge an overwhelming majority of all the votes—forty-eight for him, seventeen for Judge Hise, and seven for John C. Mason, a former congressman from Bath County. On December 12 the legislature made it official with a vote of eighty-one for Breckinridge and fifty-two for Joshua F. Bell, a Danville attorney who had made a good race as the "Opposition" candidate for governor.

Soon after the senatorial election Breckinridge traveled to Frankfort. There in a speech lasting an hour and a half, he thanked the General Assembly and declared before the men who best knew the facts that his election involved no deals and no commitments on his part. He also responded to a series of questions that had been addressed to the senatorial candidates by a group of legislators friendly to Guthrie. In so doing he took a forthright stand on the principal issues then agitating the country and his party. Quoting and commending Chief Justice Taney's opinion in the Dred Scott case, he vigorously asserted the right of slaveholders to protection of their slave property in all the territories of the United

States. Resting on the authority of the Dred Scott ruling, he thus took a more extreme position regarding the rights of slaveholders in the territories than he or his party had taken in 1854 or in 1856 or than Douglas could possibly take. At the same time he stopped short of the stand some southern fire-eaters were taking. He thought that federal courts could and would protect the rights of slaveholders in the territories; thus no federal legislation for this purpose was now required, and he did not anticipate that such a need would develop.

Breckinridge spoke against the backdrop of alarm and indignation aroused in the slaveholding states by John Brown's raid at Harper's Ferry only two months earlier. Again he devoted much of his speech to denouncing the Republican party. Quoting its 1856 platform and the speeches of Sen. William H. Seward, he argued that its tendency was to sever the bonds of brotherhood between the sections and that its ultimate purpose was to abolish slavery throughout the land. "The triumph of [their] principles," he warned, "would subvert Southern society and desolate one of the fairest regions of America." Even the more moderate aims of the Republicans, he argued, were subversive of both the Constitution and the Union. Should the Republicans gain control of the government at Washington, he feared that some states of the lower South would withdraw from the Union. Deprecating such a course, he exclaimed, "God forbid that the step shall ever be taken!" He promised that Kentucky, and he as her spokesman, would fight the Republican program within the Union and by constitutional means. He admonished the South to obey and help to enforce the laws against the foreign slave trade. It should also "frown upon, and punish all illegal expeditions, fitted out within our borders to invade feeble neighboring states. . . . Then, having placed herself in an invulnerable attitude, the South thoroughly united, will be in a condition to make a solemn and final appeal to all the better elements in the Union," particularly the northern Democrats. For Kentucky the orator pledged that the state would "cling to the Constitution while a shred of it remains."

Early in January Breckinridge returned to Washington, where he was sharing a house on G Street between Fourteenth and Fifteenth with Senator Powell and two Kentucky members of the House of Representatives, John W. Stevenson and Henry C. Burnett, and their wives. Shortly thereafter the Democracy of Kentucky again convened at Frankfort to choose delegates to the national convention at Charleston, to draft a platform, and to name presidential electors.

The platform, adopted after much maneuvering, was one on which Breckinridge could appropriately have been recommended for the presidency. On the question of slavery in the territories, it fully adopted the position of his Frankfort speech. But with no open opposition on the floor, the convention recommended Guthrie "as one upon whom all the conservative elements, . . . North and South might consistently and successfully unite." This recommendation was a compromise between the Guthrie men, who had wanted the Kentucky delegates to Charleston positively bound to support their favorite, and those who would have preferred instructing the delegates for Douglas or Breckinridge or leaving them "uncommitted and uninstructed." When the convention chose its four delegates at large, it named Guthrie stalwarts, defeating such a zealous Breckinridge supporter as James B. Clay. But those delegates selected by congressional districts included some men who favored Douglas and others whose real preference was for Breckinridge.

During the months remaining before the convention assembled at Charleston, Breckinridge made no overt effort to secure the nomination. Writing on January 30 to his Uncle Robert, he took a gloomy view of the national scene and of his own prospects.

I find my name a good deal discussed in connection with the Presidency, yet I have neither said or done anything to encourage it—and am firmly resolved not to do so. I do not think that I will be nominated, for except what is intimated in the letter of Mr VanDyke I know of no organization for me any where, and many of the friends of other gentlemen are actively whistling me down the wind. . . . I am astonished at the indifference I feel to the personal aspect of the matter.

At the age of thirty-nine the vice president could well afford to wait his turn until 1864, 1868, or even 1872. But his political friends did not practice the indifference which their idol professed. And leading figures in the Democratic party, including some by no means friendly to Breckinridge, believed or feared that he had a good chance of nomination. As the time for the national convention approached, Breckinridge asked Clay "as a personal favor to him," to go to Charleston to guard his interests and honor. Other Kentuckians, including Powell, Magoffin, Burnett, and Preston, now minister to Spain, joined him in the same mission.

In view of the size and determination of the Douglas following at Charleston, the vice president's chances for the nomination would have been meager even if he had enjoyed the hearty support of his own state convention and the delegation which it had chosen. The prospect of his nomination became still more remote when most of the delegates from the lower South walked out of the convention. The walkout took place after the convention rejected their demand for a platform declaring it the "duty of the Federal government, in all its departments, to protect, when necessary, the rights of persons and property in the Territories"—the so-called slave code plank. The Kentucky delegation, to the weary end of the balloting, gave its 12 votes to Guthrie. At one point, with the support of the Buchanan administration, he attained a total of 66½ votes to Douglas's 151½. Breckinridge had handicapped his managers by firm instructions that while Guthrie remained in the race his own name must not be allowed to come before the convention. Thus when an

Arkansas vote for the vice president was announced on the thirty-sixth ballot, Beck rose to ask that it be withdrawn. The request was honored. Others of Breckinridge's spokesmen worked earnestly, though regretfully, to keep the North Carolina delegation from turning to him while Guthrie remained a candidate.

On May 3 the remaining members voted to recess the convention until June 18 at Baltimore. During the recess the Republicans, passing over their most distinguished and most denounced leader, Seward, nominated ex-Whig Abraham Lincoln of Illinois and Hannibal Hamlin, ex-Democrat from Maine, for president and vice president. Earlier a Constitutional Union party, consisting largely of ex-Whigs and American party men, had nominated for those offices Sen. John Bell of Tennessee and Edward Everett of Massachusetts.

Meanwhile Breckinridge's attitude changed somewhat. Writing late in May to Clay, he said, "I have some hope, but no great confidence in the general result at Baltimore. If we can unite, *we will elect the nominees.* Lincoln will not run well east of the mountains. It is clear the party cannot be united on D[ouglas]." He thought it possible that he was indeed the person on whom the Democracy might unite; certain of the recent supporters of R. M. T. Hunter and Joseph Lane were reported eager to concentrate southern votes upon him. Breckinridge still felt that Kentucky should continue to support Guthrie if New York, Pennsylvania, and New Jersey, or any two of them, did so. But he urged that if it became apparent that his own real strength in those delegations and in the South was actually greater than Guthrie's, there was no further reason why Kentucky should not shift to him.

When the time for balloting was reached at Baltimore, however, the situation was far from what Breckinridge had envisioned. The Douglas men, supported by the New York delegation, had voted successfully to seat pro-Douglas contingents, newly chosen from Alabama and Louisiana, to supplant men who had withdrawn from the Charleston convention. Thus they precipitated a fresh secession, in which ten of the twenty-four Kentucky delegates took part. Most of the delegates upon whom Breckinridge's friends had depended were accordingly no longer on hand to make an effort on his behalf. The Douglas forces were in full command of the remnant of the convention; the handful of votes cast for Breckinridge and Guthrie was hardly a token.

With those Kentuckians who withdrew from the Douglas-dominated convention went most of the southern delegations which had seceded at Charleston, additional southern members, and the administration-controlled delegates from the Pacific coast, with some of that ilk from the northeastern states, particularly Pennsylvania and Massachusetts. Assembling at the Maryland Institute, they quickly adopted a platform including the slave code plank whose rejection at Charleston had precipitated the secession of the delegates from the deep South. Almost as expeditiously, they selected their nominees. George B. Loring of Massachusetts proposed Breckinridge for the presidency, urging among other things "his devoted zeal to the Constitution and the Union." In all, 105 votes were cast. On the first count Breckinridge received 81, while 24 went to Daniel S. Dickinson of New York. One by one the latter votes shifted to Breckinridge, who was finally proclaimed the unanimous choice of what claimed to be the legitimate convention of the national Democratic party. Joseph Lane of Oregon received the vice-presidential nomination by acclamation. So rapidly did the seceders work that Douglas and Breckinridge were both nominated on the twenty-third of June.

Breckinridge was now obliged to make a hurried yet crucial decision: Should he accept or reject a nomination tendered by a fraction of his party? He was aware that his opponents would question the regularity of the convention which offered him its sponsorship. He knew that less

than half of the Kentucky delegation to the original Baltimore convention had joined the forces meeting at the
Maryland Institute. This was hardly the nomination of
which he and his friends had dreamed. Certainly he was
too experienced a politician to suppose that he had much
chance to gain a majority of the electoral votes.

He soon made his choice. The Maryland Institute convention concluded its work late Saturday night. Monday
evening, June 25, a friendly crowd, headed by a brass
band, marched up Pennsylvania Avenue, surrounded
Breckinridge's G Street residence, and called him out.
His remarks were brief. He had already accepted the
nomination, he said, but with regret at the divisions
within the party. He had approved, as necessary under
the circumstances, the proceedings of the convention at
the Maryland Institute. He had determined, before the
convention selected him as its standard-bearer, to support its action and its platform. "When I discovered,
though with regret," he continued, "that my name had
been presented to the country, it did not take me long to
determine that I would not meanly abandon those with
whom I was determined to act." Mrs. Jefferson Davis,
writing many years later, reported that Breckinridge told
her immediately after his nomination, "I trust that I have
the courage to lead a forlorn hope." The statement was
completely in character. Whatever else might be said of
Breckinridge, no one could deny that he was a man of
courage—moral as well as physical. And loyalty to his
friends and political associates was a prime element in his
makeup.

For further explanations of Breckinridge's decision one
must look elsewhere. There is evidence that he thought
of his acceptance as a necessary preliminary to the withdrawal of his candidacy, as well as Bell's and Douglas's,
in order to concentrate the opposition to Lincoln on a
single candidate. Twenty years later Jefferson Davis
wrote that he proposed this step to each of the three
nominees. According to Davis, Breckinridge and Bell

agreed; Douglas refused on the ground that only he could keep his northern Democratic followers from turning to Lincoln.

In any event, none of the nominees withdrew. And Breckinridge entered upon a candidacy less wearing physically than that custom imposes upon a twentieth-century nominee, yet filled with anxiety and vexation. Tradition, seldom broken before the 1860 campaign, decreed that a presidential nominee remain at home and refrain from speechmaking on his own behalf. With minor exceptions Breckinridge followed this pattern.

On July 6 he addressed to Caleb Cushing of Massachusetts, chairman of the Maryland Institute convention, a letter formally accepting the nomination. A week later he started for Kentucky. At Baltimore and Wheeling admiring crowds demanded a speech; in each place the nominee gave a short talk, urging loyalty to the Constitution and stressing the equal rights of the states. By July 18 he had reached Frankfort, where a special state Democratic convention was in session. That evening he was serenaded and he gave another short talk of the same type. Then and there he made it clear that he expected to do no more speaking until after the election. Aside from short personal excursions, he actually did remain decorously at home in Lexington. The exigencies of the campaign led him, however, to give one full-length address, despite critics who thought it unseemly for a candidate to speak out. While Douglas traveled widely, speaking in most of the large cities of the land and in many smaller ones, Breckinridge could hardly be blamed for undertaking a single serious attempt to meet the damaging charges which Douglas and others had launched against him and the party whose standard he bore.

Still another circumstance contributed even more directly to his decision. Unhappily for his candidacy, the death of the clerk of the Kentucky Court of Appeals and an election to choose his successor took place during the summer of 1860. As its nominee the Democratic convention of July 18, managed supposedly in Breckinridge's interest, selected a little-known young man named McClarty; the Constitutional Union party proposed the elderly Leslie Combs, whom Breckinridge had defeated nine years before in his first race for Congress. Douglas Democrats, given short shrift in the Frankfort convention, turned most of their votes to Combs. The campaign was short and the result apparently was a genuine surprise to Breckinridge. As late as August 3 he had written Isaac I. Stevens, chairman of the Democratic National Executive Committee, that he expected McClarty to win, though many Breckinridge supporters would vote for Combs; and that "Nothing short of a defeat by 6000 or 8000 would alarm me for November." On August 6, the election took place and the blow fell. The margin was over 23,000 votes and Combs was the victor.

This demonstration of Breckinridge's weakness in his native state was portentous. Many observers now expected him to withdraw, but he decided on another course. On August 18, fifteen of his loyal supporters in the Lexington area requested him to address the people "for the purpose of publicly vindicating yourself from the violent personal assaults made upon you since your nomination for the presidency at Baltimore." For the occasion they proposed to give a barbecue. Three days later Breckinridge formally accepted the invitation. James B. Clay offered the use of a tract of woodland upon his Ashland estate, and the barbecue was arranged for September 5.

The appointed day was warm and estimates of the crowd varied from 8,000 to 15,000 people. Though Breckinridge was unwell and could not project his voice to reach the entire audience, he enjoyed good attention through an address lasting three hours. As the invitation had proposed, the speech was essentially defensive. The speaker first disposed of some of the falsehoods used against him by the opposition—that he had petitioned for the pardon of John Brown, that he had supported Whig Zachary Taylor against Democrat Lewis Cass in 1848, and that he had favored emancipation in Kentucky in 1849. He declined even to discuss the charge that he was not a slaveholder.[1] He denied the assertion that he had spoken in 1856 and earlier in favor of the power of a territorial legislature to prohibit slavery.

This led him naturally to an exposition of the position which his wing of the Democratic party took on slavery in the territories. It stood, he proclaimed, on the principles of the Constitution as interpreted in the Dred Scott decision. Breckinridge went on to denounce Douglas. The Illinois senator, he said, had agreed that the power of a territorial legislature over slavery was a matter for the Supreme Court to decide; but after the court had made it clear that a territorial legislature had no power to prohibit or restrict slavery, Douglas had pointed out in his Freeport debate with Lincoln a means whereby a territorial legislature, by failing to pass legislation friendly to slavery, might destroy the institution within its borders.

Then at length, but somewhat inconclusively, Breckinridge attempted to shake off the oft-repeated charge, made by Douglas, Crittenden and many others, that "I, and those Democrats with whom I am connected, are a disunion organization, who seek to break up this Confederacy of States. . . . I proudly challenge the bitterest enemy I may have on earth," he declared, "to point out an act, to disclose an utterance, to reveal a thought of mine hostile to the Constitution and union of the States." He argued that the convention which had nominated him represented not only the masses of southern Democrats, but also strong elements in most of the northern states and the whole of the party in California and Oregon. To term this assemblage "disunionist" was an absurdity. Arguing that the worst disunionists were the Republicans, who would deny the constitutional rights of the southern states, he doubted that there were fifty disunionists *per se* in the entire country if one ignored the Garrisonian abolitionists. He stated that his party's position on slavery had been affirmed by the highest judicial tribunal in the world, voted to be true by both political parties in Kentucky in 1859; unanimously asserted by both branches of the Legislature, and by an overwhelming majority of the whole Democratic party in State Convention, and declared by Mr. Crittenden himself, in the most solemn form, to be not only Constitutional, but to be sound and true, essential to the rights and equality of the States.

Then he asked a rhetorical question:

Are the people of Kentucky to be made to turn their backs to-day upon principles they thought true and constitutional last year, by loud and unreasonable clamor? Are they to be driven, terrified, staggered and bewildered by idle cries of "disunion," from maintaining their constitutional rights?

The candidate was careful, as his critics quickly pointed out, to make no direct reference to the fact that many of his supporters, particularly in the lower South, were taking the position that Lincoln's election would be a legitimate occasion for the secession of their states from the Union. Nor did he answer directly the charge that the real leaders of the organization, such as William L. Yancey, by creating and maintaining a split in the Democratic party, hoped to insure Lincoln's victory and so to provide the South with a justification for secession.

Thus at approximately the midpoint of the campaign, Breckinridge took his stand and defended his party. Bearing the standard of the most pronounced proslavery faction in the running, he took a relatively moderate tone, made no threats, showed that his party's platform was endorsed by leading southern Constitutional Unionists, and reaffirmed his personal loyalty to the Union. He did not, however, succeed in quieting the fears of many who believed, as Douglas sweepingly put it, that while "all the Breckinridge men . . . [are not] disunionists," there is "not a disunionist in America who is not a Breckinridge man."

In support of the theory that the fundamental purpose

of the Breckinridge Democracy was to promote disruption of the Union, opponents urged that its ticket could not carry a single northern state. Hence, since the electoral vote of the fifteen slave states was only 120 out of a total of 303, Breckinridge could have no expectation of a victory at the polls. On the other hand, elaborate calculations were made on the chance that none of the candidates would win a majority of the electoral votes and that the election would go to the House of Representatives. There eighteen anti-Lincoln delegations, thirteen of them definitely pro-Breckinridge, would face fifteen delegations committed to Lincoln. These calculations postulated that Breckinridge or Bell or Douglas, or a fusion between two or three of them, could carry enough of the free states to deny Lincoln a majority of the electoral votes, and that Breckinridge would carry nearly all the slave states. Moreover, the Constitution required the Senate to choose a vice president from the two men having the most electoral votes if no candidate had a majority in the electoral college; in a choice between Hamlin and Lane the Senate could be depended upon to select Lane. That worthy would become president by default on March 4 if the House were still deadlocked.

All speculation ceased after the November election. Lincoln had won 180 electoral votes, Breckinridge 72, Bell 39, and Douglas 12. The winner had garnered a clear majority of all 303 electoral votes; he had carried every free state, though in New Jersey he received four electoral votes to Douglas's three. The Republican plurality in Oregon over Breckinridge and Lane was only 264 and in California only 643 over Douglas. But even if all the anti-Lincoln votes cast had gone to one of his opponents, the Rail Splitter would still have won.

In North Carolina, Florida, Alabama, Mississippi, Arkansas, and Texas, Breckinridge won a clear majority of the popular votes. In South Carolina the legislature chose Breckinridge electors. In Georgia, Louisiana, Delaware, and Maryland, Breckinridge won by popular pluralities in excess of 44 percent, though in Maryland he led Bell by fewer than 800 votes in a total of more than 92,000. He lost Virginia's 15 electoral votes to Bell by fewer than 400 votes in a total poll of more than 167,000. Tennessee, Bell's home state, gave that statesman 47.67 percent of its total vote; but Breckinridge, strong in middle Tennessee, polled 44.52 percent. Kentucky's vote may be summarized as follows:

	Popular Vote	Percentage
Bell	66,068	45.18
Breckinridge	53,146	36.35
Douglas	25,641	17.54
Lincoln	1,365	.93
Total	146,220	100.00

A little more than half of Douglas's Kentucky votes, if transferred to Breckinridge, would have given the latter a plurality and 12 more electoral votes. In Missouri, where Douglas led Bell by fewer than 500 votes, Breckinridge ran a poor third. But in every slave state and on the Pacific coast, the vote of the two Democratic nominees, taken together, constituted a substantial majority of the votes cast. Had all the popular votes recorded for the two Democratic candidates been given to a single candidate, however, he would have had only 130 electoral votes against 173 for Lincoln. One can argue, not unreasonably, that if the Democratic party had been as united in 1860 as in 1856, its nominee (if as dynamic as Douglas or as personable and "dashing" as Breckinridge) could at least have overcome the rather small margins by which the Democrats lost Illinois and Indiana in 1860. Carrying both of those states as well as those of the South and Far West, he would have won the electoral college, 154 to 149. But this argument ignores the political history of four years, not merely that of the election year.

There is no direct evidence of Breckinridge's immediate reaction to his first and only defeat for elective office. He could not fail to be chagrined at the loss of his native state and at the schism which in retrospect made that result seem inevitable. Of the thirty-five Kentucky counties which gave Bell a majority in 1860, all but three had done as much for Fillmore in 1856. The three counties which recorded a majority for Douglas in 1860 had voted for Buchanan in 1856. All except two of the thirty-six counties which polled a majority for Breckinridge in 1860 had voted for "Buck and Breck" four years earlier. But eighteen of the twenty-five counties which in 1860 returned Bell pluralities ranging from 35 to 49.8 percent had been in the Democratic column in 1856; all but three of these twenty-five recorded an actual majority of Democratic votes (Breckinridge and Douglas combined) in 1860. With insignificant exceptions the traditionally Democratic counties produced a combined Democratic majority in 1860; with few exceptions the traditionally Whig counties gave Bell a majority that year.

In eleven counties Breckinridge won really stupendous majorities (in excess of two-thirds of the votes cast). Of these counties eight were in the almost slaveless mountains of eastern Kentucky, two (Calloway and Marshall) in the traditionally Democratic Jackson Purchase west of the Tennessee River. The other, which gave its favorite a whopping 75.2 percent of its total vote, was "Sweet Owen." But in three contiguous mountain counties (Floyd, Johnson, and Pike) he polled over 90 percent of the vote.[2]

The election over, Breckinridge had three more weeks at home before going to Washington to preside over the lame duck session of the Senate. During those weeks Kentucky, like other slaveholding states, experienced a fever of excitement and indecision. Some of the vice president's friends felt that he ought to point the way for the people of the state and of the South generally, but he remained publicly silent. Meanwhile his hometown paper, the *Kentucky Statesman*, repeatedly expressed

92

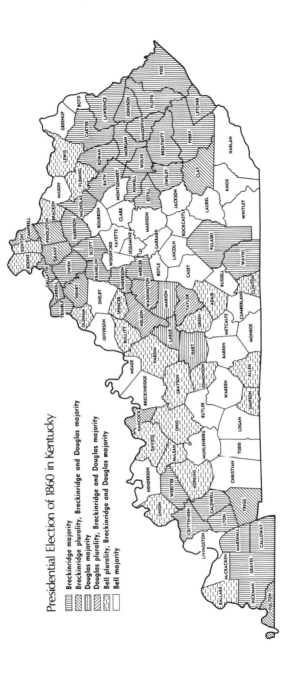

Presidential Election of 1860 in Kentucky

||||| Breckinridge majority
||||| Breckinridge plurality, Breckinridge and Douglas majority
||||| Douglas majority
||||| Douglas plurality, Breckinridge and Douglas majority
||||| Bell plurality, Breckinridge and Douglas majority
||||| Bell majority

the view that all the states should acquiesce in Lincoln's inauguration. The editor, Thomas B. Monroe, Jr., Magoffin's secretary of state, urged the cotton states to await the full unrolling of Lincoln's policy before taking action. He suggested that the states of the lower South could certainly endure the Lincoln administration as long as could the Kentuckians. He argued that with a Democratic Senate, a Democratic Supreme Court, and an anti-Republican House of Representatives, Lincoln could not hope to carry out his party's platform, so long as the southern states remained in the Union. As late as December 4 the editor felt that circumstances did not warrant calling a special session of the legislature. Writing from Washington on December 15, however, he spoke out for summoning the legislature to provide for a state convention. On December 27, Governor Magoffin issued the call for January 17.

Meanwhile on December 6, Breckinridge's good friend Powell had introduced into the Senate a resolution calling for a special committee of thirteen "to consider that portion of the President's message relating to the disturbances of the country." After extended debate the resolutions were adopted on December 18. Two days later, as the South Carolina convention adopted its ordinance of secession, the vice president appointed an able committee, representing every major faction. Included were his old friends, Douglas and Rice (the latter, now a senator from Minnesota, had supported Breckinridge in the recent election). With Bigler of Pennsylvania, also a Breckinridge supporter, they represented the northern Democrats. The five Republicans selected included Seward, now personally inclined toward compromise, and Breckinridge's onetime comrade at the Burlington bar, Grimes of Iowa. Powell of course was chairman, and the venerable Crittenden, whose compromise proposals were with numerous others referred to the committee, represented the Constitutional Union bloc. A third border state committeeman was Democrat Hunter of

Virginia. Toombs of Georgia and Jefferson Davis represented the lower South.

By the year's end the committee's work was done. On
December 31 it reported its inability to agree upon a
recommendation. The Crittenden resolutions proposed
revival and incorporation into the Constitution of the
Missouri Compromise provision regarding slavery in the
territories. This provision would have prohibited slavery
in those territories north of 36°30' while requiring Congress to protect it in territories south of that latitude. It
was rejected by the five Republican committeemen, who
followed the counsel of the president-elect. Davis and
Toombs likewise voted against the compromise, though
there is evidence to indicate that they would have gone
along with a committee majority had the Republicans
been willing to support the measure. On January 16 the
Senate itself in effect rejected the Crittenden proposals,
though efforts to pass a similar package continued until
March 4, the last day of the session.

Even earlier Breckinridge, who viewed the Crittenden
Compromise as the most extreme concession which the
southern states could possibly make on the slavery issue,
concluded that Congress would prove unable to adopt
any Union-saving program acceptable to the South.
Writing on January 6 to Magoffin, he broke his self-imposed silence and commended the governor for calling a
special session of the legislature. Attacking the negative
attitude of the Republicans in Congress, he wrote: "The
dominant party here, rejecting everything, proposing
nothing, are pursuing a policy which, under the name of
'enforcing the laws' and 'punishing traitors,' threatens to
plunge the country into all the calamities of civil war." To
halt the drift toward war, he proposed that the legislature
call a state convention. It was important, he believed, to
demonstrate the falsity of the opinion that Kentucky and
other southern states were divided about the use of force
against the seven or eight states on the verge of secession.
"I desire," he wrote,

that Kentucky may have an opportunity to determine, in the most solemn manner, her judgment of her rights, and her attitude in the present condition of affairs. . . . Let her have the opportunity, through her chosen representatives, of deciding upon the prospect of reuniting all the States in a constitutional Union, or, if that shall be impossible, let her be in a position to determine her own destiny.

In this message Breckinridge favored the step urged in other slave states by secessionists—namely, the summoning of a sovereign convention newly chosen by the voters. Such a convention, some urged, could commit the state to a course of action with an authority which the legislature, elected without reference to the existing crisis, could not. But the strong Unionist element in Kentucky was unwilling to surrender the destiny of the state into the hands of a convention which might, in a moment of excitement, adopt the extreme remedy of secession. One of the most influential of the Kentucky Unionists who strenuously opposed calling a convention was the vice president's Uncle Robert, who had publicly defended him and supported his candidacy during the presidential campaign. The legislature, which had elected the younger Breckinridge to the Senate fifteen months earlier, was now aligned much more closely with his uncle than with him. Early in February it refused by a substantial majority to call a convention. Once more the vice president's lead was rejected.

Meanwhile seven states of the lower South held conventions, all of which adopted ordinances of secession. Their representatives, meeting at Montgomery, Alabama, on February 8, adopted a provisional constitution for the Confederate States of America. The next day they elected Jefferson Davis president and Alexander H. Stephens of Georgia vice president of the new confederacy. Davis's inauguration took place on the eighteenth.

Five days earlier Breckinridge, with characteristic dignity and respect for constitutional forms, had presided over a tense joint session of Congress for the official count of the electoral votes. Wild rumors had predicted that the session would be violently broken up and even that the vice president would somehow sabotage the count. Instead he consulted with General Scott, who took the precaution of posting troops around and even inside the House Chamber. When a southern congressman made a point of order objecting to the presence of "the Janizaries of General Scott," Breckinridge firmly refused to sustain him and ordered the count to proceed. When it was over he announced in a strong, clear voice that Abraham Lincoln had been duly elected president. On February 24 he paid a courtesy call on Lincoln at Willard's Hotel.

When inauguration day came Breckinridge administered the oath of office to the new vice president, Hannibal Hamlin, who presently did the same for him and the other new senators. As a senator Breckinridge gained a forum which he had lacked as vice president; he now felt entirely free to speak on the issues of the day. With the aid of political friends in Kentucky, he proceeded to block out a new line of policy. Writing from Washington on March 10 to James B. Clay, he was apprehensive lest "patchwork" measures "make the separation eternal and leave the border states helpless." He proposed that Kentucky take the stand "that all troops should be withdrawn from the Confederate States, so that peace in any event may be *really* the policy." Then, in the guise of a request for Clay's opinion, he sketched a fivefold program:

No coercion in any form;
No Middle Confederacy—
No little end of a Northern Confederacy for Ky—
A thorough settlement which will reunite all the States, or a
    united South; . . .
If Va proposes a convention of the border slave States, the
    members from Ky should be directly from the people or
    pledged to something like the foregoing propositions.

97

This outline served as the senator's platform during the rest of the special session of the Senate and after his return home at the end of March. Thus he urged that the Senate advise the president to withdraw all federal forces from the seceded states, "where their presence can accomplish no good, but will certainly produce incalculable mischief." He warned the Senate that the border slave states would make the cause of the lower South "their own" if the federal government used force against the Confederate States. In what he must have known was a futile exercise, he stated the minimum essentials of a program for reuniting the broken Union and retaining the slave states of the border. These were to be found, he still urged, in making all the territories safe for the slaveholder with his slaves, or at least in granting an "equitable or even an inequitable division of the Territories." Finally he warned the Senate clearly of what it might expect from Kentucky:

She will exhaust all honorable means to reunite these States; but if that fails, . . . turning to her southern sisters, with whom she is identified by geographic position and by the ties of friendship, of intercourse, of commerce, and of common wrongs, she will unite with them to found a noble Republic, and invite beneath its stainless banner such other States as know how to . . . respect constitutional obligations and the comity of a confederacy.

The special session came to an end on March 28, and Breckinridge hurried home. Reaching Lexington, he quickly accepted an invitation to address the legislature, which had already received counsel from ex-Senator Crittenden. Breckinridge in his turn spoke for two hours on April 2. He reiterated his love for the Union of states under the Constitution, which he regarded as creating a limited confederacy of equal states, not a "popular consolidated government," and he made clear his belief that states might for adequate cause withdraw from the Union. Again denouncing the refusal of the dominant Republicans at any stage of the crisis to consider any reasonable measure of compromise to restore the Union, he felt that Kentucky should still attempt its restoration. To this end he proposed a conference of border slave states. The conference, he believed, should offer both the North and the lower South a plan of conciliation consisting of the Crittenden Compromise as clarified by the Powell amendment, which made the guarantees of protection to slavery in the territories south of the Missouri Compromise line specifically applicable to territory subsequently acquired. Along with this positive approach, he decried the tendency of what his less restrained supporters called the "Union Shriekers" to insist on the preservation of the Union without guarantees for the safety of the remaining slave states. Such a solution, he said, would leave the border states a helpless appendage to a northern confederacy, compelled to assist in subjugating their sister slave states and even to adopt emancipation within their own borders.

Again Breckinridge considered what Kentucky should do in the event that her best efforts to achieve a peaceable reunion were fruitless. Under such circumstances, he reasoned, she would be "free to pursue whatever course her people may think consonant with her interest and her honor." Whatever that course might be, he urged that it should be adopted only by a decisive majority. Finally he again made it clear, though in guarded terms, that he saw as a possible last resort Kentucky's union with the Confederate States.

Two days following Breckinridge's address the legislature adjourned after calling the convention of border slave states which he had urged. The Union Democrats and the Southern Rights, or States Rights, party both chose candidates for election to that convention. The States Rights party, drawn largely but by no means exclusively from the Breckinridge Democracy, chose most of its nominees from that group. General Butler and James B. Clay, as candidates for delegates at large, headed the ticket; the Union slate was led by Crittenden and Guthrie. The canvass began at once, and Breckinridge took the stump to present his case to the voters.

But again the progress of events changed the framework of decision. In the midst of the electoral campaign came the attack on Fort Sumter, Lincoln's call for troops, and Magoffin's categorical rejoinder that "Kentucky will furnish no troops for the wicked purpose of subduing her sister Southern States." Then followed quickly the secession of Virginia, the insistence of some of Breckinridge's supporters upon the immediate secession of Kentucky, and Breckinridge's own more cautious demand for a state convention to collaborate with Kentucky's congressmen in preparing a proposal to offer at the coming special session of Congress. In light of all the circumstances, of the fact that Arkansas had declined to send delegates to the border slave states convention, and most probably of a conviction that defeat was inevitable, the state central committee on April 25 withdrew the States Rights candidates.

Meanwhile Magoffin had called the legislature together once more, for a session which lasted from May 6 until May 24. At its opening he recommended that it give the people an opportunity to vote for or against summoning a sovereign convention; at the same time he urged the necessity of arming the state in its own defense. Almost immediately it was patent that the legislature still did not know what course to take, and an amazing attempt was made to provide the requisite leadership. Leaders of the Union Democrats and the Southern Rights party each appointed three representatives. These six men met at Frankfort to agree on a program which both factions in the legislature might support. Ex-Senators Crittenden and Archibald Dixon with Judge S. S. Nichols represented the Union party; Breckinridge, Magoffin, and Richard Hawes, the States Rights group. Unable to agree on the proposal of the latter for a sovereign convention, the arbitrators recommended instead a policy of neutrality and the procurement of arms with which the state might defend itself against all invaders. Neutrality caught the fancy of many Kentuckians, though the Southern Rights element was at first reluctant to accept it. In succession, however, the house of representatives, the governor, and finally the senate assented to that policy, May 16–24.

Following final adjournment of the old legislature, the political interests of Kentuckians centered first on the congressional election held on June 20, so that Kentucky might be represented in the special session of Congress which President Lincoln had summoned for Independence Day. The Union party elected nine members, while the States Rights group carried only the First District at the western end of the state. On August 5 the regular legislative elections resulted in the return of a large Unionist majority to each house of the General Assembly.

Breckinridge, who in April had urged the necessity of Kentucky's acting only by a decisive majority, could not fail to recognize that her voters were not behind him and the States Rights party. During most of the time between the two elections he was in Washington for the special session of Congress, lasting from July 4 until August 6. His course during those tense thirty-four days may be variously interpreted. There was something of the heroic about it. Almost single-handedly he attacked the war and the course of the Lincoln administration. Once more he offered his unchanged view of the Constitution as strictly limiting the powers of the federal government. His opponents charged to his face that he was a spokesman for treason; that the tendency of his arguments was to hamper the government at every turn in its efforts to preserve the Union. In his own view, he was making a record of protest against the unconstitutional measures with which the majority party was fighting an unconstitutional war. He knew that he could in no way influence the action of the Senate. Certainly if the Republicans had accepted his criticisms as valid, they would have been forced to abandon the conflict.

Asked near the end of the session what he would do, with a hostile army encamped but a few miles from the national capital, Breckinridge declared flatly,

I would have us stop the war. . . . I do not hold that constitutional liberty . . . is bound up in this fratricidal, devastating, horrible contest. . . . Sir, I would prefer to see these States all reunited upon true constitutional principles to any other object that could be offered me in life; . . . But I infinitely prefer to see a peaceful separation of these States, than to see endless, aimless, devastating war, at the end of which I see the grave of public liberty and of personal freedom.

More than once during the session Breckinridge's colleagues charged him with failing to represent correctly the sentiment of Kentucky, and they predicted that the new legislature would bring the state openly into the war under the Union banner. Certainly the results of the congressional election gave some support to their conclusion. Breckinridge, too, seemingly recognized that he might be out of step with the feeling of the majority of his constituents. He uttered no such threats as those he had voiced in March, made no predictions that Kentucky would be driven to align itself with the Confederate States. On August 1, however, he declared that

if indeed the Commonwealth of Kentucky . . . shall throw her energies into the strife, and approve the conduct and sustain the policy of the Federal Administration in what I believe to be a war of subjugation, . . . she may take her course. I am her son, and will share her destiny, but she will be represented by some other man on the floor of this Senate.

Returning to Kentucky at the session's end, Breckinridge found the other leaders of the States Rights party in a quandary following their overwhelming defeat at the recent legislative election. Still more disturbing was the fact that federal officers, backed by the senator's Uncle Robert and other staunchly Unionist Kentuckians, were now openly assembling and training a force of Union volunteers at Camp Dick Robinson, less than thirty miles south of Lexington. At a conference in which Breckinridge took part, the States Rights leaders agreed that Magoffin, who shrank from more extreme measures, should demand of Lincoln the disbandment of the troops at Camp Dick Robinson. They also inaugurated a series of anti-Lincoln picnics, to urge cessation of hostilities in the hope that the war, once stopped, could not be renewed. Breckinridge himself addressed three of the larger of these peace meetings—at Lexington, August 29, Richmond the next day, and near Mayslick, September 9. He attended a peace convention at Frankfort, September 10.

On September 3, however, Confederate forces under Gen. Leonidas Polk, denouncing the alleged violations of Kentucky's neutrality by Union troops, moved into the strongly secessionist Jackson Purchase section of the state. They were followed two days later by Union soldiers, who occupied strategic positions at Paducah and Smithland, covering the mouths of the Tennessee and Cumberland rivers. The new legislature, which had assembled on September 2, now demanded withdrawal of the Confederate forces and encouraged the movement of more Union troops into the state. On September 13 it passed over Magoffin's veto a resolution requiring the unconditional removal of Confederate troops from Kentucky soil, despite the governor's warning that adoption of the resolution would mean that it was "the purpose of the General Assembly to abandon entirely all pretence of neutrality and to commit Kentucky to active co-operation with the United States government in the prosecution of the war." On the eighteenth the legislature passed a series of resolutions which removed any lingering doubt that the majority intended to do just that.

The contingency to which Breckinridge had alluded in his Senate speech of August 1 had now arrived. The legislature had officially renounced neutrality and associated itself with the federal government's efforts to "suppress rebellion." To be consistent, Breckinridge was obliged to acquiesce in the action of an apparently large majority and certainly to resign his place in the United States Senate. But first he took a sound precaution, dictated by his own interests and the welfare of his family. He had been repeatedly warned that he was in danger of arrest and imprisonment without trial by federal authorities. Hence on September 13 he executed a deed of trust transferring all his landed holdings to a Unionist friend, attorney Madison C. Johnson of Lexington.

Meanwhile another great peace meeting scheduled to take place at Lexington on September 21 alarmed the Unionist element, which still feared armed resistance by Confederate sympathizers. From various quarters the Lincoln administration was urged to arrest Kentucky's junior senator and others of its critics. Matters came quickly to a head. On September 19, in response to the recommendation of the speakers of both houses of the Kentucky legislature, a regiment from Camp Dick Robinson moved toward Lexington with the double purpose of forestalling the peace meeting and arresting Breckinridge. The expedition, commanded by Col. Thomas E. Bramlette, paused at Nicholasville. The delay enabled a Nicholasville man to ride to Lexington and warn the senator. Sadly, Breckinridge packed a small bag, said farewell to his family, procured a mount, and during the night rode eastward with a friend. In due time he reached Prestonsburg in Floyd County. Within a few days he was joined there by such States Rights luminaries as George W. Johnson, George B. Hodge, and his Mexican War comrades, William Preston and William E. Simms. They and others proceeded on horseback across the mountains to Abingdon, Virginia, and thence by rail to Bowling Green, Kentucky. There they found Brig. Gen. Simon

Bolivar Buckner, recently head of the Kentucky State Guard, in command of an advanced Confederate position. The arrest at Louisville, on the night before Breckinridge's hasty departure from Lexington, of ex-Governor Morehead and others demonstrated the wisdom of the senator's decision not to await the arrival of Bramlette's force.[3]

It is reasonable to suppose that Breckinridge would shortly have fulfilled the pledge to resign which he made to the Senate on August 1. But he had so antagonized and alarmed the Union element now dominant in Kentucky that he could hardly have remained unmolested within the State. By driving him within Confederate lines his enemies left him no obvious alternative to joining the Confederate forces, in which his runaway son Cabell had enlisted as a private two months earlier.

In his justification and resignation, issued on October 8 at Bowling Green as an open letter to the people of Kentucky, Breckinridge added little to his previous pronouncements. He declared that the old Union was irreparably broken, that the United States as contemplated by the Constitution no longer existed, and that Kentucky was free to choose her own course. He criticized in detail the arbitrary actions of the federal government, which he had already excoriated in his Senate speeches of July and August. He attacked the Lincoln regime and the Kentucky Unionists for violating the neutrality to which the people and representatives of Kentucky had repeatedly committed her. The action of the legislature in officially ending neutrality and "throwing the State into the arms of Mr. Lincoln, to be used for Southern subjugation," he explained by the charitable supposition that the majority of its members were "actuated by a fear of military force." He took it for granted that they were no longer free agents and that in any event they had exceeded their authority. Finally he denounced the action of the federal military forces in arresting, imprisoning, or driving into exile hundreds of Kentucky citizens for speaking, writing, or even thinking in opposition to the Lincoln administration. He portrayed himself as selecting his personal course from the three alternatives of "imprisonment, exile or resistance"; not surprisingly he declared, "I intend to resist." Then he added, "To defend your birthright and mine, which is more precious than domestic ease, or property, or life, I exchange, with proud satisfaction, a term of six years in the Senate of the United States, for the musket of a soldier."[4]

The former vice president could honestly have added that his own conservative views of government had not changed—that the changes were those of the times and of the Republican party. He had been devoted to the Union of states established and governed by the Constitution. But the Union as an end to be maintained at all events, even by measures taken in violation of the Constitution as he interpreted it, would have been as unattractive to Breckinridge in January, 1859, or 1860 as in July or October, 1861. He saw the Union as a compact between equal states in which the powers of the central government were strictly limited, and in which the freedom of action and expression guaranteed to the citizen bulked large. Though he had deprecated the precipitous secession of the cotton states and doubted the possibility of peaceful secession, he never denied that a state with what it counted adequate grievances had the right to break away. At no time during his public career had he said anything which could be interpreted as endorsing the use of force to maintain or restore the Union.

5

"MUCH LOVED COMMANDER"

WITH PUBLICATION OF his open letter to the people of Kentucky, the forty-year-old ex-senator, ex-vice president turned to a military career which would occupy the next 3½ years of his life. He could not know, as he proposed to shoulder "the musket of a soldier," just what form his military service would take. But he knew that a man of his stature would not be allowed to serve as a musket-carrying soldier. On October 13 General Buckner wrote President Davis from Bowling Green, indicating Breckinridge's availability and proposing that he be commissioned a brigadier general. Buckner further recommended that he take over one of the two Kentucky brigades under Buckner's command or that he be ordered to lead a Confederate column into the eastern Kentucky counties which had given him a huge majority in the election of 1860. Breckinridge soon followed Buckner's letter to Richmond, and there on November 2 he received his commission as brigadier general. The eastern Kentucky assignment went to obese Humphrey Marshall, former Whig and Know-Nothing congressman from Louisville. Breckinridge was assigned to Gen. Albert Sidney Johnston's Western Department of the Confederate army to carry out Buckner's alternative recommendation. Accordingly on November 16 at Bowling Green he assumed command of the First Kentucky Brigade, including five infantry regiments, two artillery batteries, and a cavalry contingent. Thus the former major became responsible for leading some five thousand badly armed volunteers, most of them with a high level of dedication to the southern cause.

Almost immediately Breckinridge's position as a Kentuckian serving as a general officer in the army of the Confederate States took on a color of legitimacy. On November 18 some 200 self-appointed men, drawn from 68 of Kentucky's 110 counties, met at Russellville and organized a provisional state government. That government sought and on December 10 gained admission as one of the Confederate States of America. Breckinridge's intimate friend, George W. Johnson of Scott County, was appointed governor. A legislative council of ten men was selected to act in lieu of a legislature until it should become feasible to hold elections. Presently the council named two senators, Henry C. Burnett, who had been reelected in June to represent the First District in the United States Congress, and William E. Simms. It also chose twelve members to sit in the Confederate House of Representatives. Though the provisional government was admittedly irregular and indeed revolutionary, it professed to represent the will of the majority of Kentuckians; to Breckinridge it was the government of Kentucky for the duration of the war.

Like most officers on either side who lacked combat experience, Breckinridge would learn his new profession by practicing it. In the Mexican War he had ranked third among the officers of a volunteer regiment originally numbering about 1,000 men. He must now look forward to commanding five times that number in combat, though he had never seen a battle. Johnston himself, though a highly regarded professional soldier, had never until that autumn commanded a force of more than 3,000 men and had never handled anything like that number in combat.

So it was at the outset of the war with the high-ranking field commanders, West Pointers all, on both sides. Though Breckinridge could hardly have anticipated it, nearly five months were to pass before he, most of his men, and the commanding general were tested in battle at far-off Shiloh Church near the banks of the Tennessee River.

There on Sunday, April 6, 1862, Johnston's rebels, attacking at daybreak, surprised U. S. Grant's Union army. In mid-morning Johnston directed Breckinridge, commanding the reserve corps, to drive the Union left from the bank of the river. On unfamiliar terrain it took the inexperienced officers a long time to get their units into position. But about noon Breckinridge's men attacked and in little more than an hour they drove the enemy back ¾ of a mile. Then they encountered tough resistance from Union troops massed in what came to be called the Hornets' Nest. Shortly before Johnston received his fatal wound at about 2:15 P.M., Breckinridge called on him for help. Where Breckinridge and Gov. Isham Harris had failed, the commanding general succeeded in getting a reluctant Tennessee regiment to make one more charge. After Johnston's death Maj. Gen. Braxton Bragg took general charge of the portion of the field where Breckinridge's men were fighting. Soon after 5 P.M. the Confederate forces enveloped the Hornets' Nest and received the surrender of the Union remnant there. At 6 P.M. Breckinridge was preparing to lead another charge toward Pittsburg Landing when P. G. T. Beauregard, in overall command since Johnston's death, ordered his subordinate generals to break off the engagement.

During the first day of the Shiloh battle, the Confederates were the attackers; on the second day Grant, reinforced by two of Buell's divisions and one of his own that had gotten badly lost on Sunday, took the offensive. The fresh troops drove the battered rebels slowly back over the ground they had taken the previous day. By early afternoon Beauregard knew that the conflict was lost and that he must order a retreat. During Monday's battle Breckinridge's three brigades occupied a position near the middle of the Confederate line. There they received first the attack of Brig. Gen. William Nelson's division of Kentucky troops and then that of the Kentucky division commanded by Breckinridge's Frankfort friend and Mexican War comrade, Thomas L. Crittenden. In this harrowing episode of the Brothers' War, Breckinridge lost one of his dearest friends, Provisional Governor Johnson, whose wife was a cousin—virtually a sister—of Mary Cyrene Breckinridge.

For most of the troops on both sides, bloody Shiloh was a first experience in battle. If individual bravery and military demeanor are the tests, Breckinridge had conducted himself magnificently. Early in the afternoon of the first day, Johnston's adjutant general delivered to the Kentuckian an order to make a fresh attack. Noting that the tyro general was wearing "a well-fitting blouse of dark-colored Kentucky jeans," the staff officer later wrote, "as the order was given . . . his dark eyes seemed to illuminate his swarthy, regular features, and as he sat in his saddle he seemed to me the most impressive-looking man I had ever seen."

Most critics will agree with William C. Davis that Breckinridge had spent too much of his time leading the attacks of one of his brigades and in riding personally to carry orders or to seek orders when he might better have sent aides on these errands. But a similar charge may be made with almost equal justice against Johnston himself and all the top-ranking Confederate generals at Shiloh except Beauregard. In any case Breckinridge, like Johnston, had demonstrated to any who might have doubted it, that he possessed the first quality required of one who would command troops in combat during the Civil War—unquestioned fearlessness and complete steadiness under fire. Unlike Johnston he lived to fight again and to apply in later battles the lessons he learned at Shiloh.

Though the two-day conflict at Shiloh ended in a Confederate defeat, the reports which reached President Davis led him to recommend Breckinridge, along with B. F. Cheatham and Thomas C. Hindman, for promotion to the rank of major general; the Confederate Senate quickly confirmed the nominations. Significant is Bragg's endorsement on the order announcing the Kentuckian's promotion: "Nobly won upon the field, with . . . hearty congratulations."

During the course of the war Breckinridge served as a subordinate commander in six major battles and the campaigns leading to them—Shiloh (April, 1862) under Johnston and Beauregard; Stone's River (December, 1862–January, 1863), Chickamauga (September, 1863), and Chattanooga (November, 1863), in each case under Bragg; Cold Harbor (June, 1864) under Lee; and Winchester (September, 1864) under Jubal A. Early. During the summer of 1862 he operated in Mississippi and Louisiana under Earl Van Dorn; and in the futile Mississippi campaign of June and July, 1863, he served under Joseph E. Johnston.

Late in July, 1862, Van Dorn put the Kentuckian in command of a small task force and directed him to dislodge the Union garrison at Baton Rouge on the Mississippi. Though Breckinridge reported that malaria induced by the "climate and exposure" was "reducing regiments to companies," he delivered the attack with some 2,500 men on August 5. The miniature battle which followed was hard fought under difficulties; many of the rebels fell victims to heat prostration, though Union bullets and shells also did their work. But the small Confederate force, worn and thirsty after a grueling fifty-mile march, succeeded in overrunning the enemy's camps, destroying their stores, and driving them through the town to the river front. Five Union gunboats on the river made it impossible to hold the place, however. Shortly after the battle Breckinridge anticipated Van Dorn's orders by sending a force to occupy the bluffs at

Port Hudson, which served for nearly a year thereafter as a major Confederate bastion on the great river.

In his second battle Breckinridge demonstrated skill in planning and organization. He had learned how to use his staff effectively. Only when the death or wounding of several key officers slowed the offensive did he step in to halt an unauthorized withdrawal and to lead personally a series of assaults which brought the attack to a successful conclusion.

Meanwhile Bragg, now chief of all Confederate forces in the West, was planning an advance from the Chattanooga area into Kentucky. In this adventure he was encouraged by a small host of Kentucky refugees, eager to redeem the state from Yankee control. They assured him that the presence of a large Confederate army in the central part of the commonwealth would bring thousands of recruits to the Stars and Bars and make Kentucky an effective member of the Confederate galaxy. For obvious reasons Bragg desired Breckinridge to participate in his advance. With unusual tact he wrote on August 8,

Your influence in Kentucky would be equal to an extra division in my army, but . . . your division cannot be brought here now. To separate you from it might be injurious and even unpleasant to you, and not satisfactory to General Van Dorn. If you desire it, and General Van Dorn will consent, you shall come at once. A command is ready for you, and I shall hope to see your eyes beam again at the command, "Forward," as they did at Shiloh in the midst of our greatest success.

Breckinridge did indeed desire to take part in the expedition designed to bind his native state to the Confederate cause, but Van Dorn was reluctant to give him up. When the War Department finally ordered his release, it was too late. Before Breckinridge and the modest force which he brought with him by the roundabout railroad route from Mississippi could join Bragg, that officer had fought the Battle of Perryville on October 8. Soon thereafter he decided to abandon the Bluegrass state. News that the campaign was over and that Bragg was retreating reached Breckinridge in eastern Tennessee, only thirty-five miles short of Cumberland Gap, on October 17. Bragg presently ordered the Kentuckian to move to Murfreesboro with his troops and to take charge of the defense of middle Tennessee pending his own arrival. Accordingly Breckinridge assumed command on October 28.

Well before that date Bragg had expressed his disappointment at Breckinridge's failure to reach Kentucky and even more at the failure of Kentuckians to rise en masse to join his army. And these two aspects of his disappointment could not really be separated, for he had expected that Breckinridge's presence and eloquence would fill his Kentucky regiments with new enlistees and inspire thousands more to come forward to take their places under the Confederate banner.

Certainly the outcome of the campaign deeply disappointed Bragg, Breckinridge, and all who cherished the Confederate cause. For Breckinridge personally it had, however, one happy result. His devoted wife, who had expected to meet him in Kentucky, rode southward with the retreating troops and presently joined him at Murfreesboro. During the remaining 2½ years of the war, to the mutual comfort of both, she was with him or near him much of the time. Though her extended periods of ill health did not end with the reunion, she helped care for the wounded after many engagements, presented a flag to one of Breckinridge's Tennessee regiments, and thoroughly identified herself with her husband's men and their cause.

Bragg knew that Breckinridge's failure to join him during the Kentucky campaign was by no means Breckinridge's fault. But relations between the two men cooled rapidly after Bragg's arrival at Murfreesboro on November 30. Late in December the bitterness reached a peak. Over Breckinridge's earnest and repeated protests, Bragg insisted on the execution of Cpl. Asa Lewis of the

Sixth Kentucky regiment, whom a court martial had convicted of desertion. The corporal had not reenlisted weeks earlier with the bulk of his fellows, but had continued to do duty with his unit. He considered, however, that he was free to leave and did so when his family, in hard straits, begged him to come home. Bragg, complaining that desertions were too numerous, was determined to make an example of him. With great difficulty Breckinridge's old brigade was mustered for the execution of their comrade. Sickened as the firing squad did its nasty job, Breckinridge lurched forward in his saddle and would have fallen to the ground had not a member of his staff caught him.

Five days after the execution Bragg's army confronted Maj. Gen. William S. Rosecrans's Union Army of the Cumberland, which had moved out from its base at Nashville. On the last day of the old year and the second of the new the two armies fought one of the bloodiest battles of the war near the banks of Stone's River. On December 31 Breckinridge, holding the line east of the stream, delayed his compliance with Bragg's order to send aid to the rebels on the west side of the river. His justification was an erroneous report from Pegram's cavalry that a large Union force on the east side of the stream was advancing and threatening to fall upon his right flank. When the report was at length proved false, Bragg ordered first two and finally four of Breckinridge's brigades to Polk's assistance. When Breckinridge arrived he found that Polk had already sent in the first two brigades and that one of them in particular had been badly cut up in attempting to take a Union strongpoint. Breckinridge then personally led Preston's and Walker's brigades in another largely fruitless assault. That night Bragg ordered the whole division back to the east side of Stone's River. By noon on January 2 the Union force had occupied a wooded ridge on that bank of the river, closely paralleling the stream.

Shortly after noon, without consulting either of his corps commanders, Bragg called Breckinridge to his

114

headquarters and ordered him to take the ridge. The Kentuckian, who had made a thorough personal reconnaissance of the Union position, protested earnestly that the proposed attack could not possibly succeed, given the overwhelming strength of the Union forces occupying a parallel ridge on the river's west bank. Bragg overruled Breckinridge and gave him a peremptory order to attack at 4 P.M. To Preston the indignant Breckinridge confided that Bragg had ordered the assault over his protest. Thus Preston might testify in his friend's vindication should Breckinridge himself be killed in carrying out Bragg's order.

With courage and discipline Breckinridge's foot soldiers drove forward across the thousand yards separating them from their objective and seized the ridge. But their commander's old friend Tom Crittenden, now leading a Union corps, had massed fifty-seven pieces of artillery along the ridge west of the river. Their fire and an infantry counterattack hurled the rebels back with terrible losses. As the broken remnants of his old brigade fell back in the twilight, Breckinridge, with tears streaming down his cheeks, was heard to cry, "My poor orphans! My poor orphans!"

After the battle and subsequent abandonment of the field by the Confederate army, Bragg, seeking a scapegoat, wrote a report in which he charged Breckinridge with major responsibility for the Confederate failure. He blamed the Kentuckian particularly for delaying to send reinforcements to the west bank on the first day of the battle. He also questioned in detail the accuracy of Breckinridge's own report. Earlier the difficult commanding general had given his subordinates an opportunity to evaluate his own performance. Breckinridge, with all his brigade commanders, as well as Hardee, Cheatham, and the latter's brigade commanders, had replied by stating forthrightly their lack of confidence in Bragg's leadership.

When Breckinridge finally saw the text of Bragg's report, he requested a court of inquiry, but such an opportunity to vindicate himself never came. Meanwhile from May until September, he and most of his division served with Joseph E. Johnston's army in Mississippi. Returned to Bragg's command shortly before the Battle of Chickamauga and assigned to D. H. Hill's corps, Breckinridge and his men fought well and contributed significantly to the defeat of the Union army.

Breckinridge had now fought in three major battles, in all of which his men were called upon to take the offensive. Again his command had suffered heavy casualties; out of an effective strength of 3,769 men on the morning of September 19, he had lost almost exactly a third—166 killed, 909 wounded, and 165 missing. Again he had demonstrated his ability to inspire his men to heroic efforts while attacking against heavy odds and to adapt himself to the shifting circumstances of battle. Again his personal demeanor under fire impressed both friend and foe.

At tremendous cost in casualties the Confederates had won a great victory—indeed, their only great victory in the western theater during the war. But the victory satisfied neither Bragg nor his enemies in gray, old and new. As Bragg's numerous critics saw it, he had failed to capitalize on his success and destroy the demoralized Union army. Bragg in turn blamed several of his key subordinates (but not Breckinridge) for disobeying orders which, if obeyed, might have brought about that destruction during the prebattle maneuvering or on the battlefield itself. Taking the offensive with greater decisiveness than he had practiced during the campaign against Rosecrans, he wrote President Davis on September 25, heartily damning· one division commander (Hindman), one corps commander (Hill), and another (Polk) to whom he had entrusted the whole right wing of his army on the second day of the battle. He shortly succeeded in banishing all three from his command.

Before Hill was dismissed he joined Longstreet,

Buckner, and nine other anti-Bragg officers in signing a petition urging President Davis to remove the commanding general. Breckinridge, in view of his known feeling toward Bragg and the fact that his request for a court of inquiry was still pending, declined to sign. Hence the Kentuckian, if not restored to Bragg's good graces, was more acceptable for the moment than almost any available officer of his rank; presently he succeeded by default to the command of Hill's corps.

Meanwhile Bragg had posted his troops in a long crescent on the ridges which surrounded Chattanooga and the defeated Union army on the south and east. Early in October the Union force was strengthened by the arrival nearby of two corps from the Army of the Potomac, under the command of Joseph Hooker. On October 20, George H. Thomas, "the Rock" of Union resistance at Chickamauga, succeeded Rosecrans as commander of the Army of the Cumberland; three days later U. S. Grant, now commanding in the western theater of operations, arrived to take personal charge of the Union host. In mid-November he was further reinforced by Sherman's Army of the Tennessee.

Before the men in blue took the offensive, November 23–25, Bragg had allowed Longstreet to take nearly a third of the Confederate force with him for what proved a futile effort to dislodge General Burnside's Union army from Knoxville. Bragg was left with some 36,000 effectives, divided into two corps under Hardee and Breckinridge. As the battle for Missionary Ridge took shape, with the primary effort by Sherman directed against the northern end of the Confederate position, Hardee's corps, defending that end of the line, met the attack. Heavily reinforced at Breckinridge's expense, Hardee's men held firm. Breckinridge, who for the most part had previously fought on the offensive, was left to hold Rossville Gap and most of Missionary Ridge. With less than three small divisions he faced the whole of Hooker's and Thomas's forces. Sherman's failure and the seemingly inexplicable success of Thomas's army in storming the forbidding heights of Missionary Ridge to penetrate Breckinridge's thin lines beyond the crest are known to everyone who has read the shortest account of the action of November 25. Less well understood is the success of Hooker's troops in driving the Confederates from Rossville Gap and thus in turning Breckinridge's left flank. Overwhelming superiority in manpower gave the Union army total victory.

Bragg's career as commanding general and Breckinridge's as corps commander with the Army of Tennessee were now virtually over. In asking President Davis to relieve him, Bragg admitted that the "disaster . . . is justly disparaging to me." He strongly suggested that the true explanation of the debacle lay, however, not in his own limitations nor in Grant's numerical superiority, but in the continued hostility to him of various high ranking officers. He ascribed to Breckinridge the largest share of the blame. Bragg charged that he "was totally unfit for any duty from the 23d through the 27th—during all our trials—from drunkenness." Repeating this charge nine years later in a private letter which was not published until 1913, Bragg specified that on the night of November 25 Breckinridge came into Bragg's headquarters hut at Chickamauga Station and "soon sank down on the floor *dead drunk,* and was so in the morning."[1]

Bragg's testimony in a context of self-justification and prolonged hostility is obviously suspect. William C. Davis has recently published an extended analysis which notes many points at which independent witnesses testify to Breckinridge's vigorous performance of duty during those critical five days. He concludes that at the least Bragg's charge remains unproved.[2] One cannot deny that Breckinridge enjoyed the use of whiskey during much of his adult life. It is hard to believe that he did not fortify himself with an occasional drink during those five grueling days, particularly on the twenty-fifth, if he had the opportunity. But it seems inconceivable that Bragg, who had a long history of distrusting anyone given to excessive use of alcohol, would have retained Breckinridge in command of a corps if he had actually found him drunk on duty in any of the numerous face-to-face contacts which the two men had on November 23, 24, and 25. If Breckinridge actually collapsed on the floor during the night of the twenty-fifth, his collapse can readily be explained by extreme fatigue following long hours of stress without sleep or rest. Coming into a warm, crowded room after many hours in chilly open air might well cause an exhausted man to sink to the floor.

Though President Davis had no choice but to accept Bragg's request to be relieved as commanding general of the Army of Tennessee, he called him to Richmond in February, 1864, for assignment as his chief military adviser. Great as Davis's regard for Bragg was, he evidently took Bragg's charges against Breckinridge with a large grain of salt. For that same month he entrusted to the Kentuckian the important semi-independent command of the Trans-Alleghany or Western Department of Virginia. Less than a year later he would make him secretary of war.

During most of the period from December 15, 1863, to March 5, 1864, when he assumed command of his new department, Breckinridge was on leave. Thus he spent most of the winter in Richmond, where he was much in demand socially. But he could not forget the war and the cause which he had made his own. One of his hostesses, Mary Boykin Chesnut, recorded in her famous diary a day in January when "he walked up and down my small drawing-room like a caged lion." On that occasion he told the diarist that "the Army of the West desire the Negroes freed and put in the ranks. They wonder it has never been done before."[3] Less than three years after the establishment of a southern republic designed in large part to protect the institution of Negro slavery, Breckinridge and some of his fellow officers were convinced that the institution must be sacrificed to win independence. So far had the revolutionary situation moved the erstwhile defender of the constitutional rights of slaveholders.

In taking over the Trans-Alleghany Department, Breckinridge succeeded Maj. Gen. Samuel Jones, in command there since December, 1862. Like his predecessors, Jones had been unable to protect the area from Union cavalry raids. Influential citizens of the department had long demanded his relief. In notifying Jones of his impending replacement, Secretary of War James A. Seddon frankly stated President Davis's belief that it would be advantageous to fill the place with "an officer of distinction in the Western army, who has political as well as military influence to aid his administration."

Breckinridge's new assignment was no bed of roses. The boundaries of the department were not clearly defined, but his mission was sweeping. It had four principal aspects: (1) protecting the vital Virginia and Tennessee Railroad from Bristol to Lynchburg; (2) protecting the mines in Wythe County which were the Confederacy's principal source of lead for ammunition; (3) protecting the vital salt works at Saltville, northeast of Abingdon on the line between Washington and Smyth counties; (4) preserving the whole area as a source of foodstuffs and forage for Lee's army. The department was highly vulnerable: federal raids might be expected through numerous passes from eastern Kentucky or the Kanawha Valley.

Preparing to carry out his far-reaching responsibilities, Breckinridge made a 400-mile trip of inspection by horseback. Thus he found that at the end of March he had at his disposal some 6,110 men actually "present for duty." Their five principal elements were dispersed over an area stretching from Warm Springs to Saltville, a distance of about 150 miles. For instance Breckinridge's ranking subordinate, Brig. Gen. John Echols, commanded an infantry brigade and a cavalry regiment, numbering together about 1,800 men, stationed on the Greenbrier River south of Lewisburg.

Though one of Breckinridge's missions was to protect a vital source of supplies for Lee's army, he found the area so stripped that he was hard-pressed to feed either men or beasts. For a time a principal part of the scant rations of some of his men was provided by grinding corn the quartermaster had procured for the horses. Reporting all these circumstances in late April to Bragg, of all people, Breckinridge could boast that by denying furloughs he had increased the number of troops present for duty by almost exactly a thousand men between March 31 and April 20. But most of his cavalrymen were still dismounted, since their horses were in pasture some distance south of the Virginia and Tennessee Railroad; indeed, Breckinridge had not yet been able to procure arms for all the riders. At the end of April, Buckner, temporarily commanding the Department of East Tennessee, on orders from Richmond, sent Brig. Gen. Gabriel C. Wharton with a small brigade up the Virginia and Tennessee to Breckinridge.

Thus in early May, with the growth of fresh grass on which his horses might feed, Breckinridge's command was almost ready to make a fair showing in a defensive campaign against federal troops already advancing from the Kanawha Valley. But on May 5 he received orders from Lee to undertake a different kind of campaign. With most of his infantry and artillery, he was to join the small body of cavalry under Brig. Gen. John D. Imboden, which was scouting Maj. Gen. Franz Sigel's Union army near Winchester. Breckinridge was to take command and resist Sigel's threatened push up the Shenandoah Valley toward Staunton and possibly through the Blue Ridge passes against Lee's left flank. Leaving his chief cavalry officer, Brig. Gen. Albert G. Jenkins, in command of his department, the Kentuckian pushed Echols's and Wharton's troops toward Staunton.

Late on May 8 Breckinridge and his staff reached Staunton after riding 145 miles in three days. On the tenth and eleventh his footsore infantrymen arrived. On the twelfth the Corps of Cadets of Virginia Military Institute, some 261 men strong, joined Breckinridge's own small force.

Meanwhile Sigel had been advancing up the valley in slow stages, annoyed by Imboden's small force of about 1,600 men, which managed during the first fortnight in May to put nearly a third of the German-American's cavalrymen out of action. By May 12 Imboden was encamped just south of New Market, some forty-five miles northeast of Staunton on the macadamized valley pike. On the thirteenth Breckinridge's men moved out from Staunton and about daylight on the fifteenth they reached Imboden's camp. There Breckinridge learned that Sigel's advance force occupied the village of New Market.

Lumping together the men from his own department, the V.M.I. cadets, and Imboden's troopers, Breckinridge now commanded some 4,800 men.[4] He had eighteen pieces of artillery, including two rifled guns served by the cadets. About half of Imboden's cavalrymen were assigned to fight dismounted with Wharton's brigade. Breckinridge's first plan was to await the attack of Sigel's troops. When that attack did not materialize by mid-morning, he determined to take the offensive.

The action of that rainy, muddy Sunday fell into four phases. In the first, aided significantly by effective use of his artillery, Breckinridge's infantry, deployed in three echeloned lines, drove Sigel's men out of the village and back to a strong position on Bushong's Hill. This action began about noon.

Next rearranging his infantry in two skimpy lines with the V.M.I. cadets in reserve, Breckinridge moved out about 2 P.M. in the second phase of the battle. Spurning convention, he used his artillery almost in lieu of skirmishers, personally supervising their advance down the valley pike and stopping them repeatedly when a favorable position was found for delivering effective fire on the Union position. Under this attack and that of the advancing infantrymen, Sigel's first and weakest line of battle soon crumbled.

The third and crucial phase of the conflict followed at once as the Rebels charged up Bushong's Hill to dislodge Sigel's artillery and his second line of infantry. In the center of the Confederate line nearly half of the men of the Sixty-second Virginia Regiment were killed or wounded within a few minutes; the Fifty-first Virginia on its left was also halted. With his center shattered and with no other reserves available, Breckinridge reluctantly threw in the V.M.I. cadets just in time for them to take position behind a fence and help repel a counterattack mounted by three federal regiments. The Rebels then formed for a further charge in which the whole line—the cadets doing their part and more—fought its way up the muddy slope and drove the Union troops from the hill. But Breckinridge was not yet satisfied. Reacting to the complaints of those who had criticized Bragg for failing at once to follow up his gains at Perryville and Chickamauga, the Kentuckian drove his men in pursuit until they had exhausted their ammunition and Sigel's main force had taken position on Rude's Hill, five miles north of the battlefield.

After a pause during which his ordnance wagons came up with a fresh supply of ammunition, Breckinridge pushed off again some time after 5 P.M. in the fourth phase of the battle. Again his artillery advanced down the pike. As the Confederates reached the crest of Rude's Hill they saw the last of the Union troops crossing the bridge over the badly swollen north fork of the Shenandoah River. Presently the federal rearguard fired the bridge and effectively ended the pursuit.

Outnumbered on the actual battlefield by approximately 6,300 to 4,000, Breckinridge had won a significant victory, though admittedly against a very inept federal commander. Sigel claimed that he had been overpowered by a numerically superior Confederate force and he retreated thirty-two miles down the valley to Strasburg. The Union high command, unimpressed by his excuses, made short work of him; on May 19 he was replaced by Maj. Gen. David Hunter.

But Breckinridge deserves full recognition for seizing and keeping the initiative, for using his artillery in an innovative manner, for pressing the attack and then the pursuit to a complete victory. Except for Imboden's mounted troops, he made fullest possible use of all the men at his disposal. The battlefield was small enough to enable him to supervise the whole operation effectively; and he was close to the fighting men, encouraging them by his presence, orders, and example. One of his new subordinates summed it up succinctly:

General Breckinridge had few if any superiors on the field of battle. Besides being a man of wonderful courage, he had a keen eye to discern the strong and weak points of the enemy's position, skill in using his forces to the best advantage, and a celerity of movement which reminded me of Jackson.

May 15 was surely the finest day in his military career.

As battles go, New Market was a small affair. But it was bloody enough. Breckinridge's casualties amounted to about 530, while the Union army lost 841 men, killed, wounded, or captured.[5] Breckinridge won golden opinions from the men whom he commanded in battle for the first time as well as from General Lee himself. The latter, in response to Breckinridge's modest telegram reporting his victory, replied tersely, "I offer you the thanks of this army for your victory over General Sigel." Imboden, scouting Sigel's retreating force, closed a message on May 19 with these words: "May new honors crown you in all the future is the sincere wish of myself and little command, whose hearts you have so completely won." The Confederacy had a new hero; some thought, a new Stonewall Jackson. As the Richmond *Whig* put it, "General Breckinridge seems to be following the example of our great Jackson. He marches rapidly and whips the enemy in detail."

Breckinridge's division was next called to reinforce Lee himself, who needed every available man to counter Grant and Meade's spring offensive. Now reduced to 2,600 men—infantry and artillery—Breckinridge was in position at Hanover Junction, a good 145 miles from New Market, by May 20. Soon embodied in Lee's shifting lines, he and his men fought bravely at Cold Harbor, June 2 and 3. There Breckinridge suffered his only serious injury of the war when his horse was killed by a solid shot. As "Old Sorrel" fell, the general was pinned to the ground and bruised so severely that he could neither ride nor walk for several days.

Meanwhile Hunter mounted a new threat in the valley. On June 5 at Piedmont, a few miles northeast of Staunton, he thoroughly whipped the inadequate force with which the Confederates attempted to halt him. As soon as the news reached Lee, he ordered Breckinridge with his division to the rescue. Though the Kentuckian could not yet walk or ride a horse, he could travel by rail. On June 10 at Rockfish Gap in the Blue Ridge west of Charlottes-ville, he took command of the survivors of the June 5 disaster as well as the men he had brought with him. Hunter, heavily reinforced on June 8, proceeded farther up the valley. On June 15 he crossed the Blue Ridge south of Buchanan and moved eastward toward Lynchburg. The same day Breckinridge returned to that city and on the sixteenth his weary force of infantry and dismounted cavalry marched in.

On the twelfth Bragg had called to President Davis's attention the inadequacy of Breckinridge's force for the task at hand. "It seems to me a pressing necessity," he wrote, "to send at least 6,000 good troops to re-enforce Breckinridge." When the suggestion reached Lee the same day, he more than complied by ordering Lt. Gen. Jubal A. Early and his II Corps, about 8,000 strong, to the rescue. But Lee's far-ranging vision saw the expedition as no merely defensive operation. With Breckinridge's troops and his own, Early was to destroy Hunter's force if possible and then to clear the valley, push into Maryland, and threaten Washington. Thus Lee hoped to end the threat presented by Hunter's army and also to divert large numbers of Union troops from his own front.

Early and the advanced elements of his corps reached Lynchburg just in time to save the city. After some skirmishing Hunter concluded erroneously that he was now outnumbered, and he began a rapid retreat. Early pursued him for sixty miles until he turned off through the mountains toward Lewisburg. As the pursuit began, June 19, Breckinridge, who still could not walk, found that he could now ride horseback. So he accompanied Early throughout the three-day pursuit.

Abandoning the chase, Early gave his footsore infantry a day's rest near Roanoke, while his wagon train and artillery came up. He also made a crucial decision. Lee had given him a choice of returning to his army or carrying out the original design—clearing the valley, crossing into Maryland, and threatening Washington. Though nearly half of his infantry lacked shoes, Early began his march on June 23. At Staunton on the twenty-seventh he reorganized his army, putting Breckinridge in command of a corps consisting of his own men and Maj. Gen. John B. Gordon's division—in all about 6,800 effectives. Counting all arms, the whole expeditionary force numbered no more than 15,000 men. But with few exceptions they were hardened veterans.

The campaign unfolded according to design. Union troops made only one serious effort to halt the expedition. On July 9 near Frederick, Maryland, where the Baltimore & Ohio Railroad and the turnpike crossed the Monocacy River, Breckinridge's corps fought its way across the stream, turning the left flank of the Federal force and compelling its hasty retreat. By the evening of July 11 the expedition faced the formidable Washington defenses from the north. After consulting Breckinridge and his division commanders, Early determined to attack in the morning. But when morning came the weak defending force had been strengthened by the arrival of two fresh army corps. Early, who was daring but not foolhardy, now decided to withdraw, and by July 16 his force was safely back in the Shenandoah Valley.

Now followed two months during which Early and Breckinridge, marching and countermarching through the lower reaches of the valley, gave an impression of far greater numerical strength than they possessed. At the same time they diverted from Lee's front nearly three times as many Union troops as Early commanded. They repeatedly cut the line of the vital Baltimore & Ohio Railroad and preserved the greater part of the valley as a source of forage and foodstuffs for Lee's army. But their success could not last. In August young Philip H. Sheridan assumed command of the Union troops in the area. His mission was to drive off Early and to devastate the valley, rendering it useless as a source of supply for the rebel army. Taking his time, he reorganized his troops and familiarized himself thoroughly with the situation. Then, before dawn on September 19, he moved in overwhelming strength to carry the war to the Confederates, north and east of Winchester.

In a day of desperate fighting, Early's little army was thoroughly beaten. In mid-afternoon "Old Jube" received an erroneous report that the federal troops had turned the right of his lines and he regretfully ordered a general withdrawal. Upon learning that the report was false, he cancelled the order, but it was too late. The retreat could not be stopped, though Breckinridge and Gordon made a desperate effort to rally the Confederate left. As Gordon recalled in his reminiscences many years later, Breckinridge's

Apollo-like face was begrimed with sweat and smoke. He was desperately reckless, the impersonation of despair. He literally seemed to court death. Indeed to my protest against his unnecessary exposure. . . . he said, "Well, general, there is little left for me if our cause is to fail."

So the whipped army fled through Winchester to rally south of the town and to retreat to Fisher's Hill, twenty-five miles distant. Early had lost nearly 40 percent of his force, which numbered perhaps 12,000 men at the beginning of the day. He now lost Breckinridge. A day after the arrival at Fisher's Hill, Breckinridge received orders from Richmond, directing him to return to southwestern Virginia to take command of his old department, now combined with that of eastern Tennessee.

Throughout the campaign, Breckinridge had served the ungainly, austere, profane, and abrasive Early as a trusted counsellor and friend. The two leaders, who had first met east of Richmond late in May and who were as different in manner and personality as two men could be, built during their three months together a friendship which endured until Breckinridge's death. Each affably took from the other jibes which almost no one else would have dared address to either. On an occasion in August Early deemed it necessary to withdraw to Fisher's Hill. All was silence as the generals and their staffs rode along. Suddenly Early, a vigorous opponent of secession until his native Virginia seceded, challenged his second in command. "Well, Breckinridge, what do you think of our rights in the territories now?" As W. Stoddard Johnston, Breckinridge's adjutant general, later reported the incident, "The inquiry was so humorous and in a vein so much in contrast with the gloomy feelings of the company, that General Breckinridge and all present were thrown into good spirits at once."

During the last autumn and winter of the Confederacy, Breckinridge handled his difficult assignment about as well as anyone could. With a tiny and shifting force he sought against tremendous odds to defend the vital salt works and lead mines of southwestern Virginia, the line of railroad from eastern Tennessee to Roanoke, and the rich valley farms of eastern Tennessee and southwestern Virginia. In this forlorn hope he repelled in early October Brig. Gen. S. G. Burbridge's raid on Saltville. In mid-November, with an unbelievably small force, he outflanked an advanced Union contingent at Bull's Gap, Tennessee, under Brig. Gen. Alvan Gillem, and drove it back nearly to Knoxville.

In December Union Maj. Gen. George Stoneman planned and executed an invasion of Breckinridge's bailiwick by a two-pronged expeditionary force, one party advancing from Knoxville and the other through Cumberland Gap from Kentucky, to a junction in northeastern Tennessee. Either party was superior in numbers and in equipment to the force which Breckinridge could lead against it. Nevertheless, Breckinridge fought the united invaders to a standstill in a two-day battle near Marion, Virginia, a week before Christmas. And he abandoned the field only when his ammunition gave out. Three days later, freshly supplied with ammunition, he was advancing rapidly upon Stoneman when that officer, now in turn short of ammunition, abandoned the campaign. Stoneman's men had, however, damaged the railroad, done a good deal of mischief at the salt works and the lead mines, and destroyed important quartermaster stores at Bristol and Abingdon.

By that time the politician-general with no combat experience had thoroughly learned his new profession. He had won the friendship and admiration of Beauregard, both Johnstons, Lee, and Early, as well as such intermediate commanders as Hardee, D. H. Hill, and Polk, each of whom at one time commanded a corps or wing of which Breckinridge's division was a part. The only superior officer with whom he had any difficulty was Bragg, but Bragg's tendency to quarrel with his associates and subordinates was notorious in both the old army and that of the Confederacy.

Breckinridge, like other men who hold responsible secondary positions, was properly concerned with the judgments his superiors expressed upon his performance. Another and in some ways more significant sort of evaluation comes from subordinates—enlisted men and junior officers. There can be no doubt that Breckinridge earned the respect, admiration, and affection of the men whom he commanded. In May, 1863, when he was transferred to Mississippi, his Kentucky troops made it clear that they wished to go with him wherever he might go, even though they mistakenly believed that Bragg was again about to lead the rest of the army into Kentucky. More pointedly, after the debacle at Missionary Ridge, the men of Breckinridge's old brigade demonstrated their undiminished confidence in his leadership by seeking to be transferred with him when he finally took leave of the Army of Tennessee in February, 1864. Indeed as that army awaited the opening of the spring campaign, many of the men were still agitating to be transferred to his new department. Before he departed, the other brigades in his division expressed their feeling by presenting him with a fine dress sword inscribed, "A mark of esteem and admiration for their much loved Commander."

In reporting and explaining the military achievements of a major general without professional training as a soldier, it is not necessary to claim that he would have succeeded as the commanding general of a major army or even in directing a full-sized army corps in battle. Breckinridge's military fame rests fairly on his performance as a division commander, as the commander of a small combat force (notably at Baton Rouge, New Market, and Bull's Gap), and as the head of an undermanned geographic department. On this basis one can accept his biographer's considered judgment that no Confederate major general who was not a professional soldier before 1861 made a more creditable record.

Though Breckinridge became an effective—even a spirited and inspiring—commander in battle, he was too humane to become reconciled to the killing and maiming which are inevitable concomitants of war. The perceptive

130

Major General John C. Breckinridge, C.S.A., 1864
Courtesy of Culver Pictures

Mrs. Chesnut got a glimpse of his feeling as he escorted her home in the moonlight at three o'clock one morning in February, 1864. They had enjoyed amateur theatricals at one stately Richmond home and a sumptuous dinner at another. As they walked along the diarist said, "You have spent a jolly evening." "I do not know," was Breckinridge's reply as she recorded it. "I have asked myself more than once tonight, 'Are you the same man who stood gazing down on the faces of the dead on that awful battlefield? The soldiers lying there stare at you with their eyes wide open. Is this the same world?' "

The last phase of Breckinridge's military service to the Confederate States brought him the office of secretary of war and the awesome responsibilities which went with it in the final weeks of the crumbling Confederacy. When James A. Seddon resigned the office on January 19, 1865, after more than two years of thankless service, Davis turned to Breckinridge. On February 6 the president nominated him for the vacant place, and the Senate at once unanimously confirmed the nomination. The same day, yielding to overwhelming sentiment in Congress, he appointed Lee general-in-chief of all the Confederate armies. On the seventh the new secretary took the oath of office and went to work.

If Breckinridge did not that day realize that the cause he served was hopeless, he soon learned the truth. His conversations with Assistant Secretary of War John A. Campbell and the oral and written statements of his bureau chiefs gave him one side of the story. Telegraphic reports which the department received from Lee and the harassed commanders of other forces still in the field also revealed a shocking state of affairs. Most portentous perhaps was the treasury's inability to furnish funds to pay troops, buy supplies, or reimburse the shattered railroads for moving men and materiel. Sherman's army was cutting a wide swath of destruction across South Carolina. As that army approached the North Carolina line, Lee day by day had to report the desertion of hundreds of his hungry, cold, and unpaid soldiers, particularly those from the Old North State.[6] All devices for filling the depleted ranks had failed.

Almost immediately after he took office, Breckinridge received from Lee an ominous letter. The general-in-chief stated that the right wing of his army had been "in line of battle" beyond Hatcher's Run for three days, that "some of the men had been without meat" for all of that time, that "all were suffering from reduced rations and scant clothing, exposed to battle, cold, hail and sleet," and that his chief commissary had "not a pound of meat at his disposal."[7] Confronted by this report, the ineffective commissary general of subsistence, Col. Lucius E. Northrop, had no suggestion for a solution and actually blamed Seddon and Lee for the situation. Though Northrop had been kept in office by President Davis in spite of the complaints of every Confederate general—Breckinridge included—who had commanded a military department or an army in the field, the new secretary now quickly gained the president's consent to his removal. On February 15 the bumbling commissary general was replaced by Brig. Gen. Isaac M. St. John, previously the efficient chief of the Nitre and Mining Bureau. St. John somehow managed significantly to improve the flow of food, at least to Lee's army. Had Breckinridge done nothing more as secretary of war than end Northrop's career as commissary general, he would have deserved the applause of all friends of the Confederacy.

By the second week of March at the latest Breckinridge concluded that there was no hope for the southern cause. He now urged that the Confederacy "should surrender as a government," not piecemeal, army by army. Like Lee, he had no patience with those who would have allowed the troops who remained under arms to break up into small bands of guerrillas. Conferring with a number of senators from Virginia, Kentucky, Missouri, and Texas, he concluded, as George G. Vest, Kentucky-born senator from Missouri, remembered it ten years later, "This has been a magnificent epic; in God's name let it not terminate in a farce."

As March wore on the news became worse. By the twentieth it was clear that Joseph E. Johnston, recalled at Lee's request four weeks earlier to command in North Carolina, could not prevent Sherman's overwhelming force from going where Sherman chose to send it. Other Union armies were on the move in eastern Tennessee, Alabama, and Virginia, northwest of Richmond. By April 1 Breckinridge knew that the evacuation of Petersburg and Richmond could no longer be delayed. On the morning of Sunday the second, Lee wired the secretary, who was pacing back and forth at the War Department, that he would be forced to withdraw from his lines that night and that the capital must in consequence be abandoned. That afternoon the president and his cabinet decided to continue the government at Danville, Virginia. Breckinridge spent the rest of the day arranging the necessary transportation, including the train which was to carry Davis, the cabinet, other functionaries, and the remnant of the Confederate treasury to Danville over the dilapidated tracks of the Richmond and Danville Railroad. Late that evening the train pulled out.

The secretary of war remained overnight in the nearly abandoned capital. Soon after dawn on April 3, after a sad parting from his ailing wife, he mounted and rode across the bridge to Manchester. He had hardly passed when the bridge was fired by the last Confederate troops to leave the city. Now, accompanied by St. John, Quartermaster General A. R. Lawton, and his own former adjutant, Lt. Col. James Wilson, a recently exchanged prisoner, Breckinridge headed westward in the wake of Lee's army. During the night of April 5–6, after sundry adventures, he reached Lee's temporary headquarters near Farmville. He left Lee on the morning of the seventh; on the eighth in a dispatch to Davis he portrayed the desperate straits of the fleeing army.

When Breckinridge finally reached Danville on April

11, he learned that the president, concluding correctly that the place would soon be overrun by federal troops, had moved on to Greensboro, North Carolina. Earlier that day Davis had received news, which Breckinridge now confirmed, that Lee had surrendered at Appomattox Court House on the ninth.

At Greensboro Davis and the remaining members of his cabinet discussed the situation with Generals Johnston and Beauregard, who thought that nothing was to be gained by continuing the struggle. Davis, who still deemed it feasible and desirable to do so, was supported only by Secretary of State Benjamin. Overborne by the advice of Breckinridge, the two field commanders, Secretary of the Navy Mallory and Postmaster General Reagan, Davis reluctantly dictated a letter to Sherman, which Johnston signed and dispatched. It proposed a cessation of hostilities "to permit the civil authorities to enter into the needful arrangements to terminate the existing war."

The result of this letter was an extraordinary interview on April 18 between Sherman for the one side and Johnston and Breckinridge for the other. Johnston had proposed that the secretary of war take part in the negotiations; Sherman declined to receive him as a cabinet minister but agreed to his presence as a major general. The meeting started with a lubricating drink of Sherman's whiskey, a welcome beginning for the two parched Confederates. After a long discussion in which Breckinridge participated freely and eloquently, Johnston and Sherman signed a cease-fire agreement. Subject to the approval of higher authority on each side, it provided for the disbandment of all the Confederate armies, the recognition of the existing state governments when their members should take the oaths "prescribed by the Constitution of the United States," the reestablishment of federal courts in the South, a generous guarantee to Southerners of their constitutional rights as to person and property, and a general amnesty to take effect when all the Confederate authorities had carried out their part of the agreement.

Davis, who meanwhile had moved from Greensboro to Charlotte, decided, on the advice of all his remaining cabinet members, to accept the agreement; but it was rejected out of hand by President Johnson. On April 24 accordingly Sherman gave forty-eight hours notice of the termination of the cease-fire and demanded the surrender of Johnston's troops on the same terms as those accorded General Lee. Reporting all this by telegram to Breckinridge, who had rejoined the president, Johnston asked for instructions. Breckinridge replied with a suggestion, reflecting Davis's judgment rather than his own. He proposed that Johnston move to the southwestward—presumably for a junction with Lt. Gen. Richard Taylor's army in Alabama—with all the troops who could be mounted, after he had named a rendezvous to which the rest of his command with their small arms might presently report. But Johnston, satisfied that his men would not fight again, on April 26 signed a military convention with Sherman. By it Johnston's army was disbanded on terms virtually identical with those granted Lee seventeen days earlier.

The indomitable Davis, not waiting for the results of Johnston's new interview with Sherman, set forth that day to join Taylor's army. Escorting him and his cumbersome train of ambulances and baggage wagons were five tiny cavalry brigades, including those of Basil W. Duke and William C. P. Breckinridge, son of the secretary of war's Unionist Uncle Robert. By May 2 the slender, slow-moving column, under the general command of the secretary, reached Abbeville, South Carolina. There Davis called a meeting of Breckinridge, the five cavalry leaders, and Bragg, who had joined the party the day before, in order to plan their future course. Arguing that the troopers, less than 3,000 in number, were a sufficient nucleus around which to rally the people once the current "panic" should have passed, the president soon learned

that each of the brigade commanders thought any contin-
uation of the war impossible. He inquired why they were
still in the field. They replied that the only purpose for
which they would ask their men to fight further was to
facilitate his own escape from the country. Duke, the best
informant on this conference, reported that when a final
eloquent plea failed to move the brigadiers, "Mr. Davis
rose and ejaculated bitterly that all was indeed lost. He
had become very pallid, and he walked so feebly that
General Breckinridge stepped hastily up and offered his
arm."

That evening Breckinridge authorized the five cavalry
leaders to dismiss those of their men who wished to go no
farther; about half the troopers took advantage of the
offer. At 11 o'clock he awakened the president and rode
with him and his immediate escort for some time toward a
pontoon bridge across the Savannah River. Describing
the attitude of the troops and brightening the dismal
occasion as best he could by a good story or two, he
persuaded Davis to take flight. After what proved to be his
last conversation with his chief, the secretary then
dropped back to ride for a time with the rear guard.

An hour or so before leaving Abbeville, Breckinridge
had taken charge at the local railroad station of the remnant of the Confederate treasury. On his orders Duke
procured six wagons to transport the treasure—gold and
silver coin and bullion—with a strong guard to protect it.[8]
Some time during the night a crisis arose. Many of the
men, unpaid for months even in the now worthless Confederate bills, wished to help themselves to what remained of the treasury before it should be captured by
federal troops. It took all of Breckinridge's eloquence to
frustrate their design; even so he had to agree to divide
the silver coin among the remaining men then and
there, not as he had first proposed, at Washington,
Georgia. Making the payments at a rate of $26 a man
occupied most of May 3. Even then two of the brigadiers
indicated that they and their men would go no farther

without a direct order, which Breckinridge was unwilling to give.

On the fourth the dwindling remnants of the column reached Washington, which the fugitive president had left earlier in the day. There something over $200,000 belonging to the Richmond banks was placed in the vault of a local bank and a quantity of government bullion was stored in a warehouse. The acting treasurer, on the requisition of Breckinridge and other officers, paid out various sums in gold. Breckinridge, for instance, received $1,000 and Bragg twice that amount for "transmission to the Trans-Mississippi Department." There too the secretary, in a letter to his two remaining bureau chiefs, in effect disbanded the War Department.

On the fifth, having discharged most of the men except a few hundred Kentuckians, Breckinridge reduced his baggage to what he could carry in his saddle bags. The next day, traveling westward with a detachment of William C. P. Breckinridge's troopers in a fruitless effort to distract attention from President Davis's party, his small escort encountered a much more numerous body of federal cavalry. The general advised the younger man to surrender. Then, while his cousin parleyed with the federal commander, he rode off quietly with his two elder sons, his body servant, Colonel Wilson, and a few other men.[9] His services as secretary of war and his three and a half years as a Confederate officer were over. During the next five weeks he was a fugitive endeavoring to avoid arrest and to reach a haven in the Trans-Mississippi Department or on foreign soil.

6

ANTICLIMAX:
THE POSTWAR DECADE

Dᴜʀɪɴɢ ᴛʜᴇ ꜰɪʀꜱᴛ stages of his flight, Breckinridge felt obliged to rejoin President Davis if possible. Though the general and his small party rode almost the length of Georgia between May 6 and May 11, with more than one narrow escape from capture by federal cavalrymen, he then remained nearly three days at Milltown (now Lakeland), a few miles north of the Florida border, awaiting news from Davis. On the seventh at Sandersville he sent home his son Clifton and his young aide, James B. Clay, Jr., grandson of Henry Clay and son of Breckinridge's antebellum friend, the master of Ashland. In a modest effort at disguise, Breckinridge had cut off the long, flowing mustachios which he had cultivated during the war years and which had become almost a personal banner. At Milltown on the fourteenth he learned that the president had been captured near Irwinsville four days earlier. Thereupon he dismissed all his fellow fugitives except his son Cabell, Colonel Wilson, and Tom Ferguson, a black man about twenty-one years old who had been his body servant during most of the war. With them he crossed into Florida and soon reached Madison.

Now at last Breckinridge could make his own escape his primary concern. As a member of the Confederate cabinet under indictment for treason in several jurisdictions, as a former vice president who had resigned his seat in the Senate of the United States and offered his military services to the Confederate States, he was one of the most sought-for Confederates. Should he be taken, he had every reason to suppose that he would be tried and that he might receive the ultimate punishment for what in the North was generally regarded as heinous treason. Still for four more days he hoped that he might make his way to the west coast of Florida and there find some means of reaching Gen. E. Kirby Smith, who commanded the last forlorn Confederate hope in the Trans-Mississippi theater of operations.

At Madison Breckinridge consulted Brig. Gen. Joseph J. Finegan, a Floridian whose troops had aided him at Cold Harbor. There too he met one of Davis's aides, naval Capt. John Taylor Wood, onetime commander of the CSN raider *Tallahassee,* whose name stood nearly as high as Breckinridge's on the federal list of wanted men. Wood, who had escaped by bribing his guard when the president was taken, urged that they make for the east coast and attempt to reach the Bahamas. At Madison, after procuring some necessary supplies, Breckinridge directed Cabell, who was highly allergic to mosquito bites, to leave the party and surrender to the nearest federal officer. Whatever unknown dangers might be met along the available escape routes, it was certain that hordes of hungry mosquitoes lay in wait for anyone who would cross the Suwanee River and push southward.

On May 16 the general rode off with Wilson, Wood, and faithful Tom. At Gainesville two days later they talked with J. J. Dickison, paroled Confederate colonel who knew that part of Florida perhaps better than anyone. Dickison convinced Breckinridge that there was no chance of escaping by way of the west coast. Thus by default Wood's preferred route was adopted. Sometime during the war Dickison had captured a federal gunboat and had hidden one of its lifeboats in a shallow lake near

140

the Saint John's River. This boat he offered to Breckinridge, who readily accepted it. Dickison thereupon sent three of his former soldiers to retrieve, repair, and man the boat. At the same time he detailed another man to guide Breckinridge's party to Fort Butler on the Saint John's, where they were to meet the boat and its crew.

Moving by slow stages Breckinridge and his companions reached the designated rendezvous on May 26 and found the boat and the men—O'Toole, Russell, and Murphy—whom Dickison had sent. Breckinridge was no seaman, but he could not fail to notice that the boat was no more than seventeen or eighteen feet long, and that when the seven occupants and their supplies had been put on board, it rode very low in the water. With natural misgivings he noted in his diary, "I thought it might do for the river, but it seemed a very frail thing to go on the ocean in."

For over three days the fugitives rowed generally southward up the tortuous course of the Saint John's. Along the way they arranged for a wagon and ox team to haul the boat twenty-eight miles across country from the Saint John's to Indian River. At the designated point they found the promised team, wagon, and driver. There Murphy, claiming to be the owner of the boat, received a hundred dollars in gold as his payment and left the party. The difficulties which the others experienced during a two-day portage, with the road, with the wagon which had not been designed to carry a boat, with the oxen and their owner, and with the ever-present mosquitoes and other insect pests, were manifold. Before nightfall on May 31, however, at Carlisle's Landing near the present city of Titusville, a bit north of Cape Canaveral, they launched the boat in the salty waters of Indian River, a long narrow channel separated from the Atlantic proper by only a few hundred yards of sand reef.

Three days of rowing brought the four fugitives, O'Toole, and Russell nearly to the south end of Indian River. They had planned to enter the Atlantic through

Jupiter Inlet; but fearing that it was guarded by a federal force, they found a place where the distance across the sand reef was no more than fifty yards, dragged their boat across, and set it down in the ocean. Passing Jupiter Inlet safely in the night, they landed early on June 4 about fifteen miles to the south, not far from present-day Palm Beach. Their supply of foodstuffs nearly exhausted, they replenished their larder with turtle eggs, the only food readily available, and took on fresh water from Lake Worth. After resting for some hours, they got into the boat at about 5 P.M., listened while Wood read prayers, and then headed out toward the Bahamas. But the wind held so steadily against them that they could not get out of sight of the Florida coast. So there was nothing to do but follow the shoreline southward.

One adventure now followed quickly upon another. On June 5 the fugitives saw a large steamer approaching. It proved to be a federal transport. Hastily landing, all but one of the party disappeared into the brush. The steamer passed on, but the escapees returned too soon to their boat and were spotted. The steamer put about and a well-armed boat's crew came to investigate. While Breckinridge took cover, Wood and the two Floridians rowed out to parley with the young officer in charge. Appearing as stupid as possible, they admitted that they were paroled rebels and satisfied him that they were innocently hunting, fishing, and scavenging along the coast.

Next morning the adventurers encountered a few Seminole Indians engaged in just those activities. The Indians shared their breakfast and in exchange for some of the fugitives' small supply of gunpowder they provided some flour made from ground roots. That afternoon came the coup which would prove the key to the party's successful escape from Florida. Sighting three men—federal deserters, they thought—in a slightly longer, broader-beamed, and clearly stronger boat with a permanent mast and rigging, they gave chase, disarmed the men, and at gunpoint compelled them to exchange boats. The general sweetened this act of piracy by tendering the hapless victims a twenty-dollar gold piece and returning some of their weapons. Thus provided with a considerably superior craft, Breckinridge and Wood now determined to head for Cuba.

First, however, they needed to replenish their meager supply of food and water. Accordingly on the seventh they approached Fort Dallas at the site of modern Miami, where they found a villainous-looking pack of men of every possible color and tongue. Many of them, they concluded, were deserters from either the Union or the Confederate service. Too cautious to land and put themselves in the power of such a gang, they parleyed fruitlessly for some time. Then, starting away, they were pursued by three overloaded canoes, which they repelled with some well-placed shots. Finally O'Toole, a plausible and courageous young Irish-American, returned to the settlement in one of the canoes with a supply of gold pieces. Just as his boat-mates concluded that he had been robbed and murdered, he came in sight with a much-appreciated supply of flour, ham, other provisions, some fresh water, and a keg of rum.

That evening, endeavoring to make their exit from Biscayne Bay, the runaways repeatedly went aground on coral reefs and sand bars. They managed to dislodge the boat only by jettisoning most of their newly acquired food supply and by themselves getting out and painfully pushing the craft along. Although their feet were lacerated in the process, the exhausted fugitives finally got out into the open sea. By midnight they were out of sight of land. Before daybreak on the eighth they passed through some very rough water, and all but Breckinridge and Wood became thoroughly seasick. That day and the next the sea was relatively calm, but the hot sun beat down on the exhausted men. They were now without food and reduced to a very inadequate supply of rum and water, which the general himself doled out at widely spaced intervals.

Through the night of June 9–10 the adventurers rode out a tremendous gale, in which the waves threatened repeatedly to swamp their small vessel. Wood, who himself kept the helm all through the storm, said later that he had never, in nineteen years at sea, "felt in so great peril."

On the morning of the tenth the party encountered a merchant vessel from Maine whose captain naturally refused to let such a dangerous-looking crew come aboard. Finally, however, he threw them a lifesaving keg of fresh water and a bag of hardtack. All that day Wood and his inexperienced seamen sailed on under a hot sun. They were rewarded some hours after nightfall by the sight of a lighthouse and they then set a westerly course. In the morning they sailed into the harbor of a good-sized town, which proved to be Cárdenas, Cuba. Grateful for their deliverance, Breckinridge asked Wood to read prayers once more. When at length the sailors were permitted to land, neither onlookers nor port officials could believe that their tiny craft had actually brought them from Florida. In the five weeks since their departure from Washington, Georgia, Breckinridge, Wilson, and Ferguson had traveled at least a thousand miles as hunted fugitives on horseback, on their own feet, and as part of the crew of two fragile boats.

When the weary travelers landed, a former Kentuckian then resident in Cárdenas came forward to identify the distinguished arrival and to serve as interpreter. Still the refugees were kept at the customs house until the governor-general at Havana had wired permission for them to enter his domain. Then, numerous papers having been prepared and signed, the travelers ate a light breakfast, took rooms at a hotel, and enjoyed the luxury of a few hours rest in bed. The officials at Cárdenas were now most deferential; and the local southern colony rose to the occasion, providing the escapees with new clothing, giving a dinner in Breckinridge's honor, and hiring a band to serenade him. Next morning in a private car

144

proffered by the president of the Cárdenas branch of the railroad to Havana, the travelers proceeded to a still more cordial reception at the Cuban metropolis.

Breckinridge remained in Cuba for nearly four weeks. Certainly he needed some time to recuperate from the exhausting experience of his flight to freedom and safety, most obviously to recover from the exposure, malnutrition, and dehydration he had suffered. He learned almost at once that Kirby Smith had surrendered his disintegrating army. There was therefore no point in further efforts to reach the Trans-Mississippi Department. Though at first Breckinridge seemed understandably moody and withdrawn, he, Wilson, and Wood presently spoke freely of their escape experiences to the Havana reporters for various northern newspapers. With physical recovery and the passage of days, the general was soon his outgoing self again.

Though Breckinridge had no way of knowing it, his weeks in Cuba opened a period of self-imposed exile from the United States which would stretch out to nearly four years, a time almost exactly equal to that intervening between his hasty departure from Lexington in September, 1861, and his arrival in Cárdenas. For the moment his chief concern was to meet his family in Canada. Since there was no regular communication between Cuba and British North America, he was obliged to travel first, and for the first time in his life, to England.

Before sailing on July 7, he saw to the departure of the men who had aided his escape. Wood and Wilson had already taken passage, enroute to Nova Scotia and Toronto respectively. Dividing between O'Toole and Russell his share of the money realized by the sale in Cárdenas of the escape vessel, Breckinridge arranged the first stage of their homeward passage by steamer to Mobile. He also supplied the means for Tom Ferguson's travel by the same route and furnished him with a moving letter of recommendation, praising his courage, honesty, and fidelity through years of "peril and hardship." The letter also indicated Tom's desire to travel to Tuskegee, Alabama, and if need be to Mississippi and Kentucky, in search of his mother and other relatives, whom he expected to find with Col. Jilson P. Johnson, one of Breckinridge's former aides.

Reaching England toward the end of July, Breckinridge talked with James M. Mason, lately Confederate commissioner to Great Britain, and with the chief Confederate purchasing agents. He also made a short excursion to France to confer with John Slidell and A. Dudley Mann, commissioners to France and Belgium respectively, and to enjoy "the philosophic repose" of Mann's country place, Mount Po, near Paris. With Mason he sailed from England late in August, and on September 13 at Toronto he had a joyous reunion with his wife and all his five children except Clifton.

For nearly eleven months thereafter the senior Breckinridges sojourned in Canada, spending a severe winter at Toronto and May to August at Niagara. Though they were reasonably comfortable in the rented houses they occupied at both places and found the company of other southern exiles congenial, Mary's health was still precarious and her physician advised trying the climate of France. Breckinridge believed too that study there might prove advantageous for Owen and Fannie and not unduly expensive. The young men in the family, Cabell and Clifton, were endeavoring, each in his own way, to get a start in business in the land which their father dared not enter. Little Mary, now twelve years old, returned to New York, where she had spent the previous winter in the care of a distant cousin, Susannah Waller Lees, and her banker husband.

By August the rest of the family was ready to embark at Quebec on the *Peruvian,* the steamship which had brought Breckinridge to Canada the previous summer. For nearly two years the four of them remained abroad, living as frugally as people in their position could, one gathers from Mary's letters and from an occasional entry in her husband's diary. During the two years Owen and Fannie attended school at various times in Paris, Versailles, and Vevay, Switzerland. Their mother lived most of the time in Paris or Versailles, but Breckinridge made extended visits in England and traveled to Berlin in September, 1866, to see the triumphal review of Prussian troops following the Seven Weeks War with Austria. During the fall and winter of 1867–68, he was the guest of David R. Burbank, wealthy merchant and philanthropist of Henderson, Kentucky, with whom he had shared one of his prewar purchases of land near Saint Paul. With Burbank the general made an extended trip through southern Germany, Austria, Turkey, Greece, Syria, the Holy Land, and Egypt. In February, 1868, the two wives joined the travelers in Naples for the later and less strenuous parts of the trip—nearly two months of travel and sight-seeing in Italy, with a quick visit to Austria and Prussia.

In March Breckinridge had an audience with Pope Pius IX. The general could not fail to appreciate the irony involved in such a show of respect by the nephew of three preachers who are remembered as notable baiters of "Popery." On the other hand he could recall his own record as a strong opponent of anti-Catholic bigotry, as manifested by the Know-Nothing party in the 1850s. But the buildings and ruins of Rome itself, Pompeii, and earlier in the trip, Greece and the Holy Land, had all fascinated Breckinridge. His early education in the classics, thorough grounding in the Bible, and continuing interest in history especially enhanced the pleasure of sight-seeing in those places.

On June 4, 1868, after a final 2½ weeks in England, the Breckinridges set sail for Canada. In September Owen, in charge of his brother Clifton, was packed off to Washington College at Lexington, Virginia, then enjoying its heyday under the presidency of General Lee. Traveling through New York City, the brothers escorted their younger sister back to her second home there. Already the parents, with Fannie, had settled down once more at Niagara in a cottage which they rented at five dollars a month.

At Christmas, 1868, President Johnson issued a sweeping amnesty proclamation. Shortly thereafter Attorney General William M. Evarts instructed the United States district attorneys concerned to enter a *nolle prosequi* to the pending indictments against the former vice president. Finally in February, 1869, Breckinridge and his wife quietly crossed the Niagara River bridge and traveled by rail to Baltimore. There they enjoyed a brief stay with the general's only surviving brother-in-law, the Reverend Joseph J. Bullock, and his family, as well as other old friends.[1] Then they returned to New York for a visit with little Mary, the Lees family, and some of the men, like Horace Greeley and George Shea, who had worked persistently to make the exile's safe return possible. Next came a jaunt via Washington, D.C., to Lexington, Virginia, where they saw Clifton and Owen, as well as General Lee, William Preston Johnston, and other friends. After a second stop at Baltimore and a three-day visit in Cincinnati with Washington McLean, publisher of the *Cincinnati Enquirer*, Breckinridge took the train for Lexington, Kentucky on March 9.

"At every station," according to the *Lexington Observer and Reporter*, "the train was besieged by swarms of enthusiastic admirers," but each time the returning favorite courteously declined to make a speech. It was well after dark and rain was falling when the Breckinridges reached Lexington and were driven to the home of William C. P. Breckinridge. There a large crowd of hometown friends, standing in the downpour, could not be denied, and the returnee responded to their cheers in the briefest possible manner. In words which set the keynote for the remaining years of his life, he firmly closed the door on his past as a political leader. "The tremendous events of the last eight years," he said, "have had a great tendency to deaden, if not destroy, old party feelings, and for myself I can truly declare that I no more feel the political excitements that marked the scenes of my former years than if I were an extinct volcano."

The years of exile had not been happy years for Breckinridge. In the prime of life and in reasonably good health, he was virtually unemployed. The lack of significant employment and consequent inability to support his family in a manner which he thought appropriate were quite enough to explain the frustration and restiveness he felt. Coming after the excitement of the war years, with their grave and novel responsibilities, the postwar years were lustreless indeed.

Always a social being, the former secretary of war had made the best of his situation by cultivating old friends and making new ones, particularly but not exclusively among other expatriates and sympathizers with the Lost Cause whom he met in Ontario, England, France, and Switzerland. Wherever he went he enjoyed people and they enjoyed him. After his return to Canada, the verbose and aging A. Dudley Mann wrote him from France, recounting a humorous anecdote involving a mutual acquaintance and wishing that he might have "heard that glorious laugh of yours during the interview."

The homecoming was a heartening experience for one who could not know until he experienced it how warmly his old friends and many of his former opponents would receive him. After a few days, during which he received an almost constant ovation in Lexington, Breckinridge visited Frankfort and was greeted there by a serenade and a stream of well-wishers, calling to express their pleasure at his return. Later in the month he received similar treatment in Louisville. Early in April he was the dinner and overnight guest in Danville of his Uncle Robert, leader during the war of the Unionist element in Kentucky. With Robert's son William, whose hint had brought forth a cordial invitation from the old cleric, he moved on to Harrodsburg for a visit with his old friend Magoffin and a hearty welcome by the townspeople.

Meanwhile the general, still only forty-eight years of age, received numerous requests for his services as a legal advocate and numerous offers of other employment. Several of the insurance companies which had sprung up in the South after the war offered him generous terms if he would become their chief representative in Kentucky. The trustees and the distinguished president of Washington College sought his services as professor of law or, if he preferred, English and American history. Before settling down, however, he traveled to the Northwest with a fellow investor, Dr. Paul Rankins, to assess the state of his prewar investments in that area, particularly at Saint Paul, Superior, and Basswood Island.

When he returned to Lexington late in July, he made it clear that his native place would be his home for the rest of his life. In August he resumed the active practice of his profession. At the same time he accepted a retainer as leading counsel in Kentucky for the recently chartered Cincinnati Southern Railway, which proposed to build southward through Kentucky and Tennessee. Simultaneously he ended the strenuous competition among various insurance companies for his services by agreeing to become president at an annual salary of $5,000 of the Kentucky branch of the Piedmont Life Insurance Company of Virginia. Two or three months later this company was consolidated with another concern to form the Piedmont & Arlington Insurance Company. He also agreed to serve as president of the Elizabethtown, Lexington, and Big Sandy Railroad, whose organizers proposed to build a line connecting the two named cities with the river which forms the eastern boundary of Kentucky. For this service he was also to receive an annual salary of $5,000.

As in prewar days Breckinridge was besieged with invitations to deliver addresses on almost every imaginable occasion in every corner of the South. Also as in prewar days, he accepted few of these invitations. A succession of old friends insisted, however, that he attend the Owen County fair early in October and speak to his most faithful political constituency. This invitation he could not decline; so at last he delivered a very brief public address. Alluding to the report that "Sweet Owen" had never been completely conquered during the war, he continued, "I am sure that now we all desire amity and peace." He urged his hearers to concentrate, not on the conflicts of the past, but on the opportunities of the future.

During the six years which intervened between Breckinridge's return to Kentucky in 1869 and his death in 1875, he was able to support his family comfortably and to lend substantial sums to his elder sons as they attempted to establish themselves in agriculture and business. For the future use of his wife and children he preserved most of the speculative purchases of land he had made during the 1850s in the Old Northwest. But he never again possessed a residence which he could call his own. After a period of living in hotels, principally the old Phoenix, he rented a comfortable two-story house in Lexington on West Second Street near Broadway, and there he died.

In 1869 and 1870, however, Breckinridge was a vigorous man of middle age, who could reasonably anticipate many years of activity in his profession and in his new responsibilities for railroad building. Early in 1870 he found his fifth and last law partner in the person of twenty-seven-year-old Robert A. Thornton, a Confederate veteran, Virginia born, hardly older than his own eldest son. Thornton, a handsome and able young man, had barely three years' experience at the bar when the partnership was formed.

Breckinridge's tastes, the character of his prewar practice, and his reputation as an orator brought him so many retainers as a courtroom advocate that he was able to specialize in that aspect of his profession. In a day when prosecuting attorneys regularly sought the assistance of eminent barristers in important cases, Breckinridge usually declined to serve in that capacity. In one of the last cases he tried, however, he was the principal spokesman for the prosecution in a murder trial; his cousin, William C. P. Breckinridge, was a leading attorney for the defense in the same case. As a well-paid lawyer for the defense in criminal prosecutions and on either side in a variety of civil actions, Breckinridge was often in court, at Lexington, in the neighboring county seats, and before the Court of Appeals at Frankfort. His participation in a case was almost a guarantee that the courtroom would be crowded.

Breckinridge's services as general counsel to the Cincinnati Southern Railway were quasi-political. The Cincinnati Southern, owned by the city which gave it its name, was projected in 1869 to build to Chattanooga a road which would bring the Queen City its due share of southern business. For the counties near the probable route through central and southeastern Kentucky, it promised to be an economic lifesaver. For Louisville and the Louisville & Nashville Railroad, it seemed a dangerous rival, to be crushed in its infancy. Essential to the endeavor were charters from the legislatures of Kentucky and Tennessee, unless the trustees of the proposed road should be driven, as they threatened at times, to seek a federal charter.

During the session of the Kentucky legislature which began in December, 1869, and adjourned in March, 1870, Breckinridge spent much of his time in Frankfort; in association with the trustees of the Cincinnati Southern, he engaged in a high-class lobbying effort. The campaign reached its peak on the evenings of January 25 and 31, when Breckinridge addressed joint meetings of the railroad committees of both houses of the legislature and interested audiences which crowded the House chamber in the old state house. On January 26 and February 1, Isaac Caldwell of Louisville replied on behalf of the Falls City. Though Breckinridge, after consulting his old friend Madison C. Johnson, Nestor and scholar of the Lexington bar, presented a cogent and persuasive argument, he was not successful in winning the needed votes in the General Assembly. Neither was the City

Council of Cincinnati, which in mid-February wined and dined the entire legislature in the Queen City. When the crucial vote was taken, early in March, the Senate voted 22 to 13 and the House of Representatives 48 to 44 against the charter. During the 1870–71 session, when Breckinridge personally played a helpful but less conspicuous role, the charter passed the House but not the Senate. Only in February, 1872, was it granted. Even then the trustees sought amendments, two of which were passed toward the end of the session and another early in 1873, before beginning seriously to locate the line which the railway would take. Breckinridge took only a minor part in the legislative battles of 1872 and the following year. He did help during 1873 and 1874 in persuading farmers and businessmen of Fayette County to donate the needed right-of-way through the county, or funds with which to buy it, thus forestalling the adoption of a route which would bypass Lexington.

Breckinridge was also interested in railroad connections—almost any railroad connections—which would enable Superior City, a village of only a few hundred residents in 1870, to grow to urban status and thus make profitable his and his friends' old investment in that frigid spot. His correspondence for the period is filled with numerous projects to that end and with evidence that he attempted to use his great powers of conciliation and persuasion to reconcile conflicting opinions among the "friends of Superior" as to the best course to pursue. But nothing came of these efforts during Breckinridge's lifetime.

Little more success rewarded his efforts on behalf of the Elizabethtown, Lexington and Big Sandy Railroad, the line with which he was most intimately involved and to which he devoted his primary attention during his last five years. It was obvious to anyone who knew the facts of life regarding railroad building in the decade following the Civil War that the Big Sandy would not be built solely by local men and local money. Required for success was the participation of a larger and going railroad corporation or of northern financiers or both.

Shopping around for backing of this sort, Breckinridge and his associates negotiated for several months with Collis P. Huntington of California and New York, president of the Chesapeake and Ohio, which was being pushed westward across West Virginia. Finally in June, 1871, the C. & O. bought 52 percent of the stock of the E., L., and B.S. road. James J. Tracy, an officer and director of the C. & O., became president of the Big Sandy company, with his office in New York; Breckinridge as vice president, with the same salary as before, continued as chief representative of the company at Lexington. Of the ten directors elected at the time of the transfer of control, Breckinridge and two others represented the Kentucky interest; the other seven represented Huntington and the C. & O.

That railroad was interested in the proposed line from Lexington to the Big Sandy as a link in a major trunk line running from the Atlantic seaboard to Louisville. In October, 1871, it bought controlling interest in the Louisville, Cincinnati, and Lexington Railroad, known locally as "the short line," then operating between Louisville and Lexington as well as between Louisville and Cincinnati. But Huntington and his associates knew that the counties along the route from Lexington to the western terminus of the C. & O. at Huntington, West Virginia, stood to gain economically from the construction of the road. Accordingly they insisted that the city of Lexington and the prosperous counties, Fayette, Clark, and Montgomery, at the western end of the proposed line from Lexington to Huntington, vote bonds which might be sold to pay a portion of the construction costs.

This done, a contract was let for building the first thirty-three miles of the road. On June 26, 1872, the line was opened from Lexington to Mount Sterling. For the time being, it amounted to an eastward extension of the L., C., & L.; that road leased the new line, supplied the necessary rolling stock, and actually operated it. While the road was under construction, Breckinridge was necessarily concerned with both major issues and petty details. He was harassed by people who were much exercised about the exact location of the line and of the depots at Winchester and Mount Sterling. Meanwhile he was hard at work, personally inspecting the proposed route from Mount Sterling to the Big Sandy, endeavoring to win friends for the railroad in the counties through which it would pass, and procuring, with the help of local attorneys, the necessary right of way.

Though most thoughtful Americans of the 1870s knew that there was little economic hope for a community without at least one line of railroad, they had abundant reason to doubt the altruism and integrity of the managers of many railroad corporations. Fayette County itself was already legally obligated to pay the interest and principal on bonds issued to an earlier Big Sandy railroad company, which had never constructed a mile of track. By 1873 there were plenty of grumblers in the county who suspected and said that the new Big Sandy road would never be built beyond Mount Sterling. Breckinridge's standing in the community, however, was such that many citizens believed, on the basis of his repeated statements, that Huntington and the C. & O. were genuinely interested in the E., L., and B.S. as a link in the trunk line which they projected, that they were committed in all good faith to building the road from Mount Sterling to a connection with their own line, and that it would be completed in due time.

There was a rise of confidence in October, 1872, when Huntington and other officers of the C. & O. inspected the L., C., & L., and the Big Sandy roads from Louisville to Mount Sterling. In January, 1873, Breckinridge, in a private letter to General Early, wrote that the Big Sandy road would be "finished to the [West] Virginia line by the spring of 1874" and that he expected Early to travel to Kentucky over it during the summer of that year. In April,

1873, contracts were let for building the road. In late July Breckinridge, with his old associate, General St. John, now consulting engineer for the railroad, spent a week on horseback inspecting the proposed route; he told a reporter that this would probably be the last such inspection before the completion of the road. By September another Kentucky director, interviewed on his return from a meeting of the board in New York City, reported that the road would surely be completed. He explained the current delay as a result of the difficulty, given the state of the market, in selling the bonds of the line. As late as September 10, Breckinridge, just back from New York, stated to a Lexington newspaper "his belief that Mr. Huntington is very much in earnest and anxious to build our road, and that inside of a month there will be a strong force at work."

But these expectations were dashed within a week by the failures of Jay Cooke and Company and of Fisk and Hatch, financial backers of Huntington and the C. & O. These and other failures brought on the Panic of 1873, which was followed by a prolonged depression. Before the end of the year the C. & O. defaulted on its bonds; presently it went into receivership. Nothing further could be done toward completing the road during the remaining year and a half of Breckinridge's life. Not until November, 1881, was the Big Sandy line completed; only then did the reorganized Chesapeake and Ohio run its first through train over that route to Lexington. Meanwhile in November, 1873, Breckinridge renewed his public statement of confidence in the C. & O. leadership and in the completion of the Big Sandy link. At the same time he published a letter of explanation from Huntington himself.

For the third time a financial panic and the prolonged depression which followed had occasioned embarrassment for Breckinridge. His father's death during the depths of the depression of the 1820s had left his mother and her children almost penniless. The financial situation following the Panic of 1857 had pressed him so hard that he was forced to sell his Lexington property in order to complete the expensive dwelling he had started in Washington. Unable to realize anything substantial from his western investments, he had presently been compelled to dispose of his Washington home before he occupied it. And now the Panic of 1873 made impossible the fulfillment of the repeated assurances which in good faith he had given his fellow citizens that the Big Sandy road would be completed at an early date. One can only guess what the nonfulfillment of these assurances and the need to reiterate them cost a man of Breckinridge's lofty pride.

While Breckinridge was still an exile, men as unlike as Horace Greeley and General Grant thought his return to the United States and Kentucky desirable because they believed that his influence in public affairs would be exerted on the side of moderation and reconciliation. Grant hoped that he would become governor of Kentucky, and many Kentuckians echoed the sentiment. Breckinridge's pride, however, kept him from encouraging any effort to remove his own political disabilities under the Fourteenth Amendment. Since this action was never taken, he could not have become governor even if he had wished to seek the office. But his voice and influence during the six years following his return repeatedly opposed lawlessness and unthinking glorification of the Lost Cause, while supporting peace and harmony within the state and between the sections. Thus in March, 1870, he vigorously denounced the Ku Klux Klan. His pragmatism and the extent of his adjustment to the new order are suggested by his quiet support for the 1872 Kentucky statute by which the testimony of blacks was at last made admissible in court in cases involving whites.

His hard-bitten friend Early pretended to think Breckinridge "too much imbued with 'progressive ideas' to care for the presentation" of the history of the Confederate States. Though the Kentuckian did not indulge in

157

cheap attacks—public or private—on the federal government, the new amendments to the Constitution, or the policies of Congress, he retained a self-respecting pride in the part he had played in the fight to win southern independence. So he assured his old comrade in arms, "I seek no man's society, who speaks of us as 'traitors,' nor will I associate with our former adversaries upon the basis of mere sufferance." Furthermore, unlike Early and many other Confederate chieftains, he adamantly refused to take part in or supply weapons for the war of words in which one general was glorified at the expense of another's reputation. Nor would he say or write anything which could be construed to reflect unfavorably upon the military or civil policies of Jefferson Davis.

Breckinridge's self-restraint was completely in character; it was particularly appropriate for one whose days were numbered. Though people had almost invariably been impressed by his physical presence, his manly appearance, and his fine carriage, he had never, even in youth and early manhood, been entirely healthy. In his military campaigning he had suffered occasional bouts of sickness and, at Cold Harbor, one serious injury. His arduous flight in 1865 had been preceded and followed by spells of sickness. As he grew older his resilience declined, and the incidence of illness increased.

Quite sick in the summer of 1873 after his personal inspection of the route of the Big Sandy railroad east of Mount Sterling, the general rallied in late August to attend to the business of the road in New York. In October he was sick again at home for several weeks, during which his daughter Fannie served as his amanuensis. In March, 1874, hoping to benefit from a change of climate, he and his wife visited their elder sons in Arkansas. There he saw his first grandchild and namesake, the three-year-old son of Cabell and his wife Sallie Johnson, the daughter of an old friend, Robert W. Johnson, a former senator from Arkansas. Later that spring Breckinridge was confined to his room for several weeks, completely unable to attend to any business. By late May he had recovered a little. As soon as he could travel, he and Mary found a peaceful spot at the Lees home in Westchester County, New York. There too he sought recuperation in vain. Writing from this haven on June 29, 1874, to a cousin who had consulted him about a legal problem, he reported that he had had a severe attack of pleuro-pneumonia. Though he also reported his doctor's prediction that he would be able to return to work in the fall, the old soldier had for all practical purposes reached the end of his career. Presently he went home and after October he was unable to leave the house.

In search of health he turned from one doctor to another. The last, John R. Desha, was an old personal friend. When the spring of 1875 brought no significant improvement in the general's health, two of the most eminent surgeons in the land, Dr. Lewis A. Sayre of New York, who in his youth had lived for some years in Lexington, and Dr. Samuel D. Gross of Philadelphia, were called into consultation. After a thorough examination, they agreed that the fundamental difficulty was cirrhosis of the liver, caused initially, they thought, by the general's injury at Cold Harbor. The cirrhosis had led to other complications, but the immediate problem was the patient's right lung, which they found two-thirds full of a fluid of which he often expectorated two or more quarts a day. On May 11 Sayre, with the general's hearty approval, attempted an operation designed to permit the fluid to drain through an artificial opening. Though the patient's weakness led the surgeon to stop before the operation was complete, some drainage from the incision took place and Breckinridge felt some relief. The next day two of his personal and professional friends, James B. Beck and Frank K. Hunt, assisted him in completing his will. During his few remaining days he received a succession of visitors, including Vice President Henry Wilson, whose speeches he had once quoted to illustrate the dangerous tendencies of the new Republican party.

On the morning of the seventeenth, Sayre carried out a supplemental surgical procedure to drain off more fluid, which decreased the distention of the general's abdomen and temporarily relieved the pain he had experienced. But before the afternoon was over, he began to fail rapidly and at 5:45 he died. Gathered around his bedside were his wife, his two daughters, his favorite son Clifton, his nephew Cabell Bullock, his cousin W. C. P. Breckinridge, Doctor and Mrs. Desha, and other friends and kinfolk. The object of their concern died without any recorded last words. It was just as well. Breckinridge had long since said what he wanted to say; at the end he was too weak to add more.

In Breckinridge's last six years he had industriously minded his own business and sought decently and honorably to promote his own and his community's fortunes. He had also set an example of moderation and conciliation for the many Kentuckians and Southerners generally who had learned in other days to admire or even to love him as a political leader, as a trusted military commander, or simply as a man of character and charm.

The clergyman who preached the funeral sermon, the Reverend W. F. V. Bartlett, new pastor of the First Presbyterian Church, had known Breckinridge only briefly; but he summed up a great deal of his character in four short sentences near the end of his address:

The last days of this great man were in harmony with his previous life. There was the same calmness and serenity, the same unshaken courage and fortitude, the same reticence in regard to himself. . . . He spoke freely of death as he would have done of a journey to a foreign land. He lay unmoved and calm, patiently waiting whatever Providence might have in store for him.

Though Breckinridge had requested a simple funeral, that wish could hardly be fulfilled. In a session like many in which he had participated, the Fayette County bar met to adopt resolutions of regret at his passing. Four of the men who had been his partners in the practice of law survived, and three of them—Kinkead, Beck, and Thornton—spoke. So did other lawyers who knew him as a formidable adversary. Similar tribute would have been paid to almost any Lexington attorney. But in recognition of Breckinridge's death public buildings and many business houses, both in Lexington and Louisville, were draped in black. A special train from Louisville and extra coaches on the morning train from Cincinnati brought hundreds of old army comrades and brother Masons to take part in the funeral procession. The fifteen pallbearers included men with whom Breckinridge had been closely associated in politics, in military service, in the practice of law, or in purely personal friendship. Kentucky's governor, both of the state's United States senators, and a host of other distinguished men joined the crowd in paying tribute. The First Presbyterian Church was much too small to hold those who wished to attend the funeral service; even the surrounding streets were filled with mourners. The funeral procession, more than a mile long, with General Duke as chief marshal, escorted the body to the Lexington Cemetery. Numerous veterans of the Mexican and Civil wars marched in the procession. So did ten commanderies of Knights Templar, whose members conducted their committal service at the grave.

As the procession moved up Main Street it passed under "a huge United States flag draped in black." Certainly the man whose lifeless body passed under the banner had for most of his life honored that flag and the day of his return in 1869 to the country it symbolized had been one of the happiest of his life. Whatever fault he and his friends found with the administration of the government at Washington, he died believing that it was the best government in the world.[2]

APPENDIX A: BRECKINRIDGE FAMILY GENEALOGY*

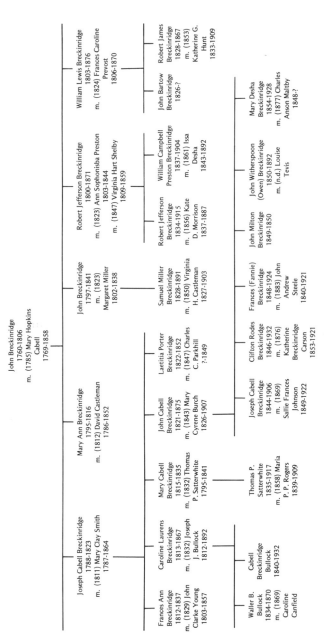

*Numerous members of the family who do not figure in the narrative have been omitted.

Appendix B:

Breckinridge's Attitude toward Slavery

THE ARGUMENT THAT John C. Breckinridge was at heart opposed to slavery rests in the first instance on the assumption that he must have imbibed and retained the antislavery views which his gradualist uncles and brother-in-law had been preaching since he was a schoolboy. It is supported by his compassionate efforts to aid a free black man whom he thought wrongfully convicted of manslaughter and by his decent, considerate treatment of his own few slaves and other blacks. It is supposedly clinched by the testimony of his onetime friend, emotional, unstable John W. Forney, that if Breckinridge "had a conscientious feeling" when the two men first met in 1851, "it was hatred of slavery."

If Breckinridge really shared the moderate antislavery views of his contentious uncles and his brother-in-law, to all of whom he was deeply indebted, he should have said so, or at least remained silent while they fought in 1849 for the emancipationist cause. It is hard to believe that he dissembled his convictions to win a ten-week term in the Kentucky legislature. Breckinridge's humane attitude toward individual black men and women was by no means unique among defenders of slavery and proves nothing regarding his views on the institution. Forney's statement is suspect, to say the least. It was published in June, 1864, when Breckinridge wore a Confederate uniform and Forney was editor of the Washington organ of the Lincoln administration.

In his one full-length speech during the 1860 presidential campaign, Breckinridge responded directly to the charge that he had been an emancipationist in 1849 or had at least sympathized with the emancipationist views of his Uncle Robert. In sweeping terms he challenged his hearers: "If there is an individual among the thousands within the sound of my voice, who ever heard or knew of my sympathizing with the doctrines advanced by Rev. R. J. Breckinridge, let him now speak, or forever hold his peace." No one spoke.

Notes

Chapter 1

1. This paragraph is based on Lowell H. Harrison, *John Breckinridge, Jeffersonian Republican* (Louisville, 1969). For the authorship of the Kentucky Resolutions, see pp. 75–81.

2. For names, dates, and ages of the Breckinridges mentioned in this narrative, see genealogical table, Appendix A.

3. Thomas and Samuel were younger brothers of Breckinridge's brother-in-law, the Reverend Joseph J. Bullock. All three were sons of Waller Bullock, owner of a rich Bluegrass farm, Walnut Hill, in Fayette County.

4. Loco Foco was the popular Whig term for Democrats generally, though it originally referred to a supposedly radical Democratic faction in New York.

5. Mary Cyrene's parents had died several years before her marriage. She was brought up by Mr. and Mrs. Milton Burch. Burch, a brother of her father, was married to Martha Viley, a sister of her mother.

Chapter 2

1. John C. Breckinridge rented a pew in his uncle's church.

2. Under the Constitutions of both 1799 and 1850, voting in Kentucky was *viva voce*.

3. William C. Davis, *Breckinridge: Statesman, Soldier, Symbol* (Baton Rouge, 1974), nevertheless argues (see esp. pp. 14, 43, 59, 163, 243) that John C. Breckinridge was at heart opposed to slavery. For a discussion of this argument see Appendix B.

4. *Kentucky Statesman*, June 14, 1853.

5. See p. 42.

6. But see the latest biography of Douglas: Robert W. Johannsen, *Stephen A. Douglas* (New York, 1973), pp. 386–410.

7. Ibid., pp. 410–34; Roy F. Nichols, *Franklin Pierce, Young Hickory of the Granite Hills* (Philadelphia, 1958), pp. 319–24, 333–8.

8. The "Hards" or "Hardshell" Democrats in general were unwilling to receive back into party fellowship the "Barnburner" faction which had seceded from the party in 1847–48 to support ex-President Van Buren's candidacy for president as a Free-Soiler. The "Softs" or "Softshell" Democrats were ready to do so.

9. Michael F. Holt, "The Politics of Impatience: The Origins of Know Nothingism," *Journal of American History* 60:315–20 (September, 1973).

10. Mary C. Breckinridge to John C. Breckinridge, Jan. 11, 1854, Breckinridge Papers (Library of Congress). The uncharitable reference is to the elder statesman's third marriage, the previous year, to a wealthy and charming widow, Elizabeth Ashley of Saint Louis. It was a marriage of genuine mutual affection. Albert D. Kirwan, *John J. Crittenden: The Struggle for the Union* (Lexington, 1962), p. 283.

11. Johannsen, *Douglas*, p. 482.

Chapter 3

1. Magoffin to Breckinridge, July 2, 1856, Breckinridge Papers (Library of Congress).

2. All quotations from the Tippecanoe speech are drawn from a draft in Breckinridge's handwriting, endorsed "Rough Draft of a Speech at Tippecanoe Ind in Sept 1856." Breckinridge Papers (Library of Congress).

3. See map, p. 65.

4. The session of the legislature which began in December, 1857, would be the last before the new senator's term began unless the governor called a special session.

5. The "constitution without slavery" option would have protected Kansas slaveholders in their continued ownership of slaves—about 200 in number—already in the territory but would have prohibited further importation of bondsmen.

6. In spite of the ambiguity, Kansans understood the issue clearly. When the vote was taken, August 2, they rejected the Lecompton Constitution more than six to one.

Chapter 4

1. The manuscript census returns of 1860 and the tax rolls of Fayette County do not show Breckinridge as a slaveholder in the election year. He had sold his Lexington home in 1857 and his Washington home on I Street, which he never occupied, in February, 1859, and made his home in Lexington at the Phoenix Hotel. Accordingly he had very little need for slaves or permanent employees of any kind.

2. See election map, p. 93.

3. Morehead was whisked away to Fort LaFayette in New York harbor. There and at Fort Warren (Boston) he was held without indictment for nearly four months.

4. When the Senate met in regular session, it took notice that Breckinridge "is now in arms against the Government he had sworn to support"; on December 4 it voted, 36–0, "that the said John C. Breckinridge, the traitor, be, and he is hereby, expelled from the Senate." Powell, Andrew Johnson, and four other Democratic senators abstained. Rice, who was absent on the fourth, appeared next day, asked the privilege of recording his vote and did so in favor of expulsion.

Chapter 5

1. *Official Records of the War of the Rebellion* (Washington, 1880–1901), ser. 1, vol. 52, pt. 2, 745–6 (cited hereafter as *O.R.*); William M. Polk, *Leonidas Polk, Bishop and General*, 2 vols. (New York, 1915), 2:306–13, esp. 313.

2. *Breckinridge*, pp. 393–9. As none of the communications in which Bragg charged Breckinridge with drunkenness during the battle was published during his lifetime, he had no occasion or opportunity to respond personally to the charge.

3. Ben Ames Williams, ed., *A Diary from Dixie* (Boston, 1949), p. 362. In these remarks Breckinridge identified himself with the revolutionary proposal outlined in a memorandum presented by Maj. Gen. Patrick R. Cleburne a few days earlier to the ranking generals of the Army of Tennessee at Dalton, Georgia. Cleburne, who saw the Confederate States losing the war for lack of military manpower, proposed to enlist large numbers of black soldiers, with freedom for themselves and their families as the consideration. Though the commanding

general, now Joseph E. Johnston, declined to forward Cleburne's recommendation to the War Department, an opponent sent a copy to Richmond. Davis and the cabinet considered it but rejected the proposal, kept it from the general public, and ordered Cleburne to do nothing more about it.

4. Excluded from this total are 500 reserves from Augusta and Rockingham counties, who were not used in the battle. William C. Davis, *The Battle of New Market* (Garden City, 1975), pp. 193–7.

5. In reporting the numbers involved and the losses on both sides and in evaluating Breckinridge's leadership at New Market, I have adopted Davis' figures and followed his analysis.

6. Lee to Secretary of War, Feb. 24, 1865, *O.R.*, ser. 1, vol. 46, pt. 2, 1254; Feb. 28, 1865, ibid., 1265.

7. Lee to Secretary of War, Feb. 8, 1865, *O.R.*, ser. 1, vol. 46, pt. 1, 381–2.

8. Duke was obliged to take charge of the treasure without knowing its value, even in general terms. The best estimate is that it still included about $290,000 in specie and bullion, plus something over $200,000 belonging to the Richmond banks. M. H. Clark, "The Last Days of the Confederate Treasury and What Became of Its Specie," *Southern Historical Society Papers* 9:542–56 (October-November, 1881); A. J. Hanna, *Flight into Oblivion* (Richmond, Va., 1938), pp. 90–2.

9. Cabell had served as an aide on his father's staff except for a short time after the Battle of Missionary Ridge, when he was held as a federal prisoner. Clifton, a naval cadet on the James below Richmond during the last months of the war, had joined his father at Greensboro, April 11.

Chapter 6

1. Breckinridge's mother, who had moved to Baltimore with the Bullocks in 1861, died there in October, 1864; his last surviving sister, Caroline Bullock, died in November, 1867.

2. Newspaper clipping in Sallie Johnson Breckinridge Scrapbook, reporting a conversation with Breckinridge. The scrapbook is in the possession of Peter Ten Eyck of Boston. I am indebted to William C. Davis for a copy of the clipping.

Bibliographical Essay

THE MOST IMPORTANT body of personal papers for the study of John C. Breckinridge is the Breckinridge Family Papers in the Manuscript Division of the Library of Congress. Other significant holdings of Breckinridge materials are found at the Chicago Historical Society, the Filson Club, Louisville, and the University of Kentucky. Particularly useful was the collection of Mr. and Mrs. John Marshall Prewitt, Mount Sterling, Kentucky, which includes the diary Breckinridge kept from August, 1866, until March, 1868. Still other important collections of Breckinridge sources are in the National Archives, Washington, D.C., and in the possession of Mrs. James Carson Breckinridge, Summit Point, West Virginia.

Collections which proved useful, either because they include letters from John C. Breckinridge or because they supply important background evidence, are the William Bigler and James Buchanan Papers at the Historical Society of Pennsylvania, Philadelphia; the Stephen A. Douglas Papers at the University of Chicago; the Thomas B. Stevenson Letters at the Cincinnati Historical Society; the Guthrie and Caperton Family Papers, the Ann Viley Johnson Papers, the J. Stoddard Johnston Papers, and the William Preston Johnston Papers at the Filson Club; the Thomas H. Hines Papers at the University of Kentucky; the minutes of the Deinologian Society, 1835–38, and scattered reports and correspondence of John C. Young in the Library of Centre College, Danville, Kentucky; the Charles Mason Diaries in the Iowa State Department of History and Archives, Des Moines; and the Bayard Papers, the Thomas J. Clay Papers, the William W. Corcoran Papers, the Jubal A. Early Papers, and the Andrew and John W. Stevenson Papers at the Library of Congress.

The essential collection of sources for the war years is the massive publication of the War Department, *The War of the*

Rebellion: A Compilation of the Official Records of the Union and Confederate Armies, 128 vols. (Washington, 1880–1901).

Among the more useful newspaper files used were those of the Burlington *Hawkeye and Iowa Patriot,* 1841–43; Burlington *Iowa Territorial Gazette and Advertiser,* 1841–43; *Cincinnati Daily Enquirer,* 1856, 1869; Frankfort *The Commonwealth,* 1841, 1858–61; Frankfort *Kentucky Yeoman,* 1847–49, 1859–61, 1869; Lexington *Kentucky Gazette,* 1840–41, 1843–44, 1870, 1873; Lexington *Kentucky Statesman,* 1849–61; Lexington *Observer and Reporter,* 1844–49, 1869–70; *Lexington Press* (tri-weekly or daily), 1872–75; Louisville *Daily Courier,* 1856, 1861; Louisville *Courier-Journal,* 1869–70, 1875; Louisville *Daily Democrat,* 1857–58; Louisville *Daily Journal,* 1860, 1868; Louisville *Daily Times,* 1852, 1856; Washington, D.C., *The Constitution,* 1860–61.

A contemporary and slanted analysis, unsigned but actually written by Robert J. Breckinridge, is "The Secession Conspiracy in Kentucky and Its Overthrow," *Danville Quarterly Review* 2 (1862):111–40, 221–47, 371–95.

Published diaries, journals, memoirs, and reminiscences which proved particularly useful include Mary Boykin Chesnut, *A Diary from Dixie,* edited by Ben Ames Williams, Boston, 1949; M. H. Clark, "The Last Days of the Confederate Treasury and What Became of Its Specie," *Southern Historical Society Papers* 9 (1881):542–56; Leander M. Cox, "Mexican War Journal of Leander M. Cox," edited by Charles F. Hinds, *Register of the Kentucky Historical Society* 55 (1957):29–52, 213–36; 56 (1958):47–70; Basil W. Duke, *Reminiscences of General Basil Duke, C. S. A.,* Garden City, N.Y., 1911; Edward A. Ferguson, *Founding of the Cincinnati Southern Railway,* Cincinnati, 1905; John B. Gordon, *Reminiscences of the Civil War,* New York, 1903; John W. Green, *Johnny Green of the Orphan Brigade: The Journal of a Confederate Soldier,* edited by Albert D. Kirwan, Lexington, 1959; John B. Jones, *A Rebel War Clerk's Diary at the Confederate States Capital,* 2 vols., Philadelphia, 1866; Ed Porter Thompson, *History of the Orphan Brigade,* Louisville, 1898; John S. Wise, *End of an Era,* Boston, 1900.

For Breckinridge's escape to Cuba in 1865, see A. J. Hanna, ed., "The Escape of the Confederate Secretary of War John Cabell Breckinridge As Revealed by His Diary," *Register of the*

Kentucky State Historical Society 37 (1939):323–33; and John Taylor Wood, "Escape of the Confederate Secretary of War," *Century Magazine* 47 (1893):110–23.

The only useful biography of Breckinridge hitherto published is that of William C. Davis, *Breckinridge: Statesman, Soldier, Symbol,* Baton Rouge, 1974. This imposing work of 687 crowded pages is the product of an imaginative and exhaustive search for source materials and of skill in assimilating the material found. Though I differ from Davis in emphasis and at points on both fact and interpretation, I am indebted to this product of Davis's assiduous labors.

A selected list of biographies which are particularly useful to the student of Breckinridge's career includes the following titles: Douglas S. Freeman, *Lee's Lieutenants: A Study in Command,* 3 vols. (New York, 1944); Lowell H. Harrison, *John Breckinridge, Jeffersonian Republican* (Louisville, 1969); Robert W. Johannsen, *Stephen A. Douglas* (New York, 1973); Philip S. Klein, *President James Buchanan, A Biography* (University Park, Pa., 1962); Grady McWhiney, *Braxton Bragg and Confederate Defeat* vol. 1 (New York and London, 1969); Roy F. Nichols, *Franklin Pierce: Young Hickory of the Granite Hills* (Philadelphia, 1931); William M. Polk, *Leonidas Polk, Bishop and General,* 2 vols. (New York, 1915); Don C. Seitz, *Braxton Bragg, General of the Confederacy* (Columbia, S.C., 1924).

The national background for Breckinridge's career in politics is best supplied by David M. Potter, *The Impending Crisis, 1848–1861* (Evanston, Ill., 1976). Other particularly useful secondary works include Henry Cohen, *Business and Politics in America from the Age of Jackson to the Civil War* (Westport, Conn., 1971); Thomas L. Connelly, *Army of the Heartland: The Army of Tennessee, 1861–1862* (Baton Rouge, 1867); Thomas L. Connelly, *Autumn of Glory: The Army of Tennessee, 1862–1865* (Baton Rouge, 1971); E. Merton Coulter, *The Civil War and Readjustment in Kentucky* (Chapel Hill and London, 1926); Ollinger Crenshaw, *The Slave States in the Presidential Election of 1860* (Baltimore, 1945); William C. Davis, *The Battle of New Market* (Garden City, 1975); Emerson D. Fite, *The Presidential Campaign of 1860* (New York, 1911); Roy F. Nichols, *The Disruption of American Democracy* (New York, 1948); Jasper B. Shannon and Ruth McQuown, *Presidential Politics in Kentucky, 1824–1948* (Lexington, 1950).

171

A selected list of scholarly articles which proved helpful includes Philip R. Cloutier, "John C. Breckinridge, Superior City Land Speculator," *Register of the Kentucky Historical Society* 57 (1959):12–19; James E. Copeland, "Where Were the Kentucky Unionists and Secessionists," ibid., 71 (1973):344–63; William C. Davis, "The Vice President Flees," *American Heritage* 24 (1973):10–11, 14–15, 80–84; Will D. Gilliam, Jr., "Party Regularity in Three Kentucky Elections and Union Volunteering," *Journal of Southern History* 16 (1950):510–18; Walter A. Groves, "Centre College—the Second Phase, 1830–1857," *Filson Club History Quarterly* 24 (1950):311–34; Charles Kerr, "Transylvania University's Law Department," *Americana* 31, no. 1 (January, 1937).